A Disciple's Path

Deepening Your Relationship with Christ and the Church

Companion Reader

James A. Harnish

Abingdon Press

Nashville

A DISCIPLE'S PATH
DEEPENING YOUR RELATIONSHIP WITH CHRIST AND THE CHURCH
COMPANION READER

Copyright © 2012 by Abingdon Press

First edition published as ISBN 978-1-4267-43504
ISBN 978-1-5018-58147. New cover printing, 2018.

(New cover printing)
18 19 20 21 22 23 24 25 26 27—10 9 8 7 6 5 4 3 2 1
MANUFACTURED IN THE UNITED STATES OF AMERICA

CONTENTS

INTRODUCTION
A Divine Discontent

Have you ever felt that there was something you wanted, something you were missing, something you needed to do but did not know how?

Have you ever had a sense that there ought to be more to being a member of the church than just attending worship, making a pledge, and sitting on a committee?

If so, then you have experienced a "divine discontent."

Whatever our religious background may be, most of us long for something more. We catch fleeting hints of a spiritual hunger for a deeper relationship with God. We know why the psalmist wrote:

> As a deer longs for flowing streams,
> so my soul longs for you, O God. (Psalm 42:1)

Wherever we are along the journey of faith, we are pestered by the realization that church should not just be where we go, but who we are.

Wherever the path of our lives is leading, when we remember Jesus said, "Follow me!" to the first disciples, we feel an inner tug to rise up and follow him too.

But how do we do that? Like disciples who have come before you, you may ask,

- How do I follow Jesus in a real and tangible way?
- What spiritual practices enable me to experience a more vibrant relationship with God?
- Where do I find the practical steps that will lead me along my own pathway of discipleship?
- What difference does it make to live out my commitment to Christ through membership in The United Methodist Church?

These kinds of questions tug at a disciple's soul when experiencing a divine discontent—when longing for a deeper relationship with Christ and the church.

That was the experience of Benjamin Ingham in March 1734. The sun had just begun to burn away the early morning frost as he made his way through Oxford to the Lincoln College apartment where he met John Wesley. Ingham came to Wesley with questions about the methods by which he and a half-dozen fellow students could develop a systematic pattern for what they called "the holy life." He had come to the right place!

Richard Heitzenrater, who discovered Ingham's diary, concluded that Wesley had a method for just about everything.[1] Ingham's diary confirms the way fellow students called Wesley and his followers "Methodist" because they were so "methodical" in the development of their spiritual lives and in their service to others, keeping watch over the most trivial details of their daily lives.

In the same way, we make our way back to Wesley to reclaim the methods by which we can live into The United Methodist Church's mission of making disciples of Jesus Christ for the transformation of the world. We come with a divine discontent for a richer, deeper, more vibrant life in Christ. Like Ingham, we've come to the right place!

A Disciple's Path grew out of that kind of divine discontent in the hearts of the staff and lay leadership of Hyde Park United Methodist Church in Tampa, Florida, when we found that many of our new members had never moved into deeper practices of spiritual discipline or found their place to serve as the agents of the church's mission in the world. It gave birth to a conviction that we were called to do more than make members. It was time to focus on making disciples. It led us to some challenging questions that every body of committed Christians should ask:

- How do we move from "making members" for the church to "making disciples" of Christ?
- How do we engage in the essential practices that enable us to grow into the likeness of Christ and become a part of God's transformation of the world?
- How do we, as growing disciples, discover our unique gifts and become engaged in transforming ministry both within and beyond our church walls?
- How do we form disciples in the unique context of our Wesleyan tradition?

That was when we turned to Wesley to find the method by which we can take our next appropriate step along the pathway of discipleship.

Wesley's Way of Disciple-making

We found our answers in two important elements of our Methodist heritage.

First, in Wesleyan theology and experience, conversion is not a one-time event but an ongoing process of transformation into the likeness of Christ. Wesley called this "the holy life." We don't just "get saved" and wait to go to heaven. God's love and grace are continually at work in our lives in a dynamic process by which we grow toward "maturity, to the measure of the full stature of Christ" (Ephesians 4:13). *A Disciple's Path* is grounded in a Wesleyan understanding of prevenient, justifying, and sanctifying grace as the way in which we are formed into the likeness of Christ.

The second answer was found in Wesley's method. He was a pragmatic leader who organized his followers around specific disciplines by which "the people called Methodist"[2] would continue to grow in the love of God.

The core of that method was the way Wesley organized his followers in small groups, originally called "societies" and later known as "class meetings."

While the student groups at Oxford took a variety of forms, they included three elements:

1) study of Scripture and a wide variety of spiritual and religious classics
2) devotional piety practiced through meditation, self-examination, prayer, and Bible reading
3) social outreach, particularly engagement with the poor, the disadvantaged, children, and the imprisoned

About *A Disciple's Path*

A Disciple's Path engages us in these two streams of our Methodist tradition. After an overview of basic United Methodist beliefs and practices (Introductory Session or Pastor's Coffee), the study combines a uniquely Wesleyan understanding of our growth in God's love and grace (Week 1) with the time-tested practices of spiritual discipline expressed in the vows of membership we profess when we commit ourselves "to participate in the ministries of the church by our prayers, our presence, our gifts, and our service and witness"[3] (Weeks 2–6). It also involves us in the practice of those disciplines in Christian community with other disciples who are walking the same path. Two resources guide you along the journey: *A Disciple's Path Daily Workbook* and *A Disciple's Path Companion Reader.*

The *Daily Workbook* provides five daily readings and reflection questions for each week of the study with space for recording your responses. This format is designed not only to teach you about the spiritual disciplines but also to help you put them into practice. Just as John Wesley encouraged Benjamin Ingham to use a journal or diary as a way of tracking his spiritual growth, it is our hope that the *Daily Workbook* will serve a similar function for you.

The *Companion Reader* you hold in your hands provides helpful background material and insights from our rich Wesleyan heritage that are designed to enhance and expand your exploration of the weekly topics. Whether you are a small-group member or a group facilitator, this book is intended to help you dig deeper into the practices by which we are formed as disciples of Jesus Christ. Each chapter corresponds to a week of study in the *Daily Workbook* and can be read during the week in preparation for the group session. This book also can be used as a free-standing resource for personal growth as well as preparation for worship, teaching, and preaching when *A Disciple's Path* becomes the basis for a congregation-wide focus on the life of discipleship. However you use it, it will prove to be a valuable tool as you seek to grow in discipleship.

"Follow Me!"

Discipleship in the Wesleyan tradition is an invitation to a new way of living in which we learn to love God with our whole hearts, minds, and strength and to love others the way we have been loved by God. That invitation is as clear and simple today as it was when Jesus called his first disciples by saying, "Follow me!" His invitation appears twenty-one times in all four Gospels. Every time Jesus says it, he calls for decisive action. His invitation always calls for active response.

And now, the invitation comes to you! It's the invitation to join Wesley and his followers in developing the patterns of spiritual discipline by which our hearts and lives are transformed by the love of God revealed in Jesus Christ. It is the path that leads to life.

> *How happy, gracious Lord, are we,*
> *Divinely drawn to follow thee.*
> *—Charles Wesley*[4]

WHY ARE YOU A UNITED METHODIST?

"Why are you a Methodist?" The question took me by surprise as I stepped into the elevator, forcing me to come up with a terribly inadequate answer. How would you respond? Why do you choose to follow Christ in the context of the Wesleyan/Methodist tradition?

The person who asked that question was a Baptist. Particularly for those of us who live in the southern United States, those denominational labels represent two major branches of Christian faith in the Protestant tradition. On one side is the Calvinist or Reformed tradition represented by many Baptists, Presbyterians, and the independent fundamentalist churches. On the other side is the Armenian or Wesleyan tradition represented by the folks like the United Methodists and Episcopalians.

The differences came home to me when *Time* magazine listed "10 Ideas Changing the World Right Now." Number three on the list was "The New Calvinism." Here's the way the writer described it:

> Calvinism is back . . . complete with an utterly sovereign and micromanaging deity, sinful and puny humanity, and the combination's logical consequence, predestination. . . . It offers a rock-steady deity who orchestrates absolutely everything . . . by a logic we may not understand but don't have to second-guess.[1]

The writer traced the Calvinist influence in America to seventeenth-century Puritans like Jonathan Edwards but went on to say, "It was soon overtaken in the U.S. by movements like Methodism that were more impressed with human will."[2]

That article came out while I was writing a review of William Paul Young's best-selling novel, *The Shack*, for the *Tampa Tribune*. I wrote that Young was in the flow of the Wesleyan tradition when he had "Papa," the African-American woman who represented God in the story, say, "Just because I work incredible good out of unspeakable tragedies doesn't mean I orchestrate the tragedies. Don't ever assume that my using something means I caused it. . . . Grace doesn't depend on suffering to exist, but where there is suffering you will find grace."[3]

The morning after that article appeared, I found a voicemail from a woman who, with tears in her voice, said, "I don't know anything about the Methodists, but I know that's what I've always believed." The conversation with her confirmed the reasons I follow Christ in the Methodist tradition.

- **I follow Christ in the Methodist tradition because of the Wesleyan balance between God's providence and human freedom.**

Methodists don't necessarily believe in a "micro-managing deity . . . who orchestrates absolutely everything." While holding to a high view of the sovereignty of God, we don't believe that "God has a reason for everything." Rather, we believe that God loves us enough to give us the freedom to reject that love. God is relentlessly at work to fulfill God's saving purpose for us while never abrogating the freedom planted within us. God intends for everyone—not just a predestined few—to receive God's saving love and redeeming grace in Jesus Christ.

Charles Wesley described God's universal love in his hymn "Come, Sinners, to the Gospel Feast":

> *Come, sinners, to the gospel feast;*
> *let every soul be Jesus' guest.*
> *Ye need not one be left behind,*
> *for God hath bid all humankind.*[4]

• I follow Christ in the Methodist tradition because of the Wesleyan balance between heart and head.

I'm grossly oversimplifying here, but it's an oversimplification that makes the point. The Reformed tradition tends to put primary emphasis on what happens in one's head. The important thing is to get the truth and get it right in the assurance that right belief in right doctrine is the critical factor in a right relationship with God. That is an emphasis we need, particularly in a time when a lot of flaky foolishness floats around under the guise of religion that doesn't pass the test of reasoned truth.

While Methodists affirm the importance of what happens in our heads, the center point of our spiritual tradition is on what happens in our hearts in the confidence that if we get our hearts right, our heads will follow. For Methodists, the heart of the matter is always a matter of the heart. Charles Wesley described it as

> *a heart in every thought renewed*
> *and full of love divine,*
> *perfect and right and pure and good,*
> *a copy, Lord, of thine.*[5]

• I follow Christ in the Methodist tradition because of the Wesleyan balance of personal piety with social action.

Eddie Fox has traveled the globe as director of World Evangelism for the World Methodist Council. When someone asks him which is more important, personal piety or social action, Eddie says that it's like breathing. Personal piety is the way we breathe in; social action is the way we breathe out. The only way to know which is more important is to ask which you did last.

Methodists have always agreed with the writer of the epistle of James that faith without works is dead. The inner transformation of the heart must be expressed through social transformation of the world in which we live. Although the actual source of the quotation is disputed, there's no question that these words often attributed to John Wesley capture the spirit of Methodism:

> *Do all the good you can,*
> *By all the means you can,*
> *In all the ways you can,*
> *In all the places you can,*
> *At all the times you can,*
> *To all the people you can,*
> *As long as you ever can.*[6]

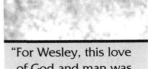

Christians in the Methodist tradition are social activists because they are convinced that the love we feel in our hearts must become the love we express with our hands. The faith we believe with our minds is expressed through engagement in the real issues of the world around us—poverty and economic injustice, racism and prejudice, violence and peacemaking, care for the environment, and the almost infinite variety of ways in which people suffer and struggle to survive.

"For Wesley, this love of God and man was neither a feeling, nor even a noun, but always a verb."
—Peter Storey[7]

The love of God made known to us in Jesus Christ must become tangible in this world through our lives.

• I follow Christ in the Methodist tradition because of the balance between present and future salvation.

We believe that God's salvation is not a static thing. It's not a form of spiritual vaccination. We don't just "get saved" and then wait to go to heaven. Wesley used the terms *sanctification* and *Christian perfection* to describe the ongoing process by which the grace of God is constantly at work in us to shape our lives into the likeness of Christ. Methodists believe that salvation is a living, growing, dynamic relationship in which God forgives and heals the brokenness in our lives so that we can participate in God's healing of the world. We'll be exploring the process of sanctification as we move through *A Disciple's Path*.

• I follow Christ in the Methodist tradition because of the method that is embedded in our heritage.

Wesley knew that no one grows into the likeness of Christ instantaneously or accidentally. God's work of grace in our lives is directly related to the practices by which we are formed as followers of Christ. In his sermon "Christian Perfection," John Wesley wrote, "How much soever any man hath attained, or in how high a degree soever he is perfect, he hath still need to 'grow in grace,' [2 Pet. 3:18] and daily to advance in the knowledge and love of God his Saviour."[8]

Methodists are methodical because we believe that it is through the practice of the time-tested disciplines of the Christian life that our lives are continually being centered in the two commandments that Jesus said are at the core of our discipleship, namely, loving God and loving others.

When John Wesley listed the characteristics that identify disciples in the Methodist tradition, he wrote:

> A Methodist is one who has "the love of God shed abroad in his heart by the Holy Ghost given unto him;" one who "loves the Lord his God with all his heart, and with all his soul, and with all his mind, and with all his strength." . . . And while he thus always exercises his love to God, . . . he accordingly loves his neighbour as himself; he loves every man as his own soul. His heart is full of love to all mankind.[9]

All of this is, of course, a more extensive answer than I could give to my friend in the elevator. But if it happens again, I have my "elevator speech" ready. I'm a Methodist because we really believe that being a Christian is all about learning to love God and love others and it provides me with a method to do that. That's why I'm a Methodist!

Why The United Methodist Church?

John Wesley said that the characteristics that marked a Methodist are "the common principles of . . . plain, old Christianity."[10] So, what is unique about being a disciple of Jesus Christ in The United Methodist Church?

At our church we regularly host a Pastor's Coffee for individuals who want to learn more about our church and how to grow in their faith. We begin by inviting each person to share three facts and a question. The facts can be anything they want to share about themselves, including how they found their way to our church. The question can be any question they bring with them about what it means to be a part of this congregation.

It's always fascinating to discover the spiritual traditions out of which people come and the questions they bring with them. The questions generally revolve around several specific areas: our history, our Wesleyan understanding of grace, our sacramental life, our United Methodist connection, and our mission.

Our History

At the Pastor's Coffee, we give participants a drawing of the Christian family tree similar to the one pictured here. It's a visual image of the history of the Christian church with all of its major denominational branches growing out of the roots that are embedded in the New Testament. We invite the ones who have

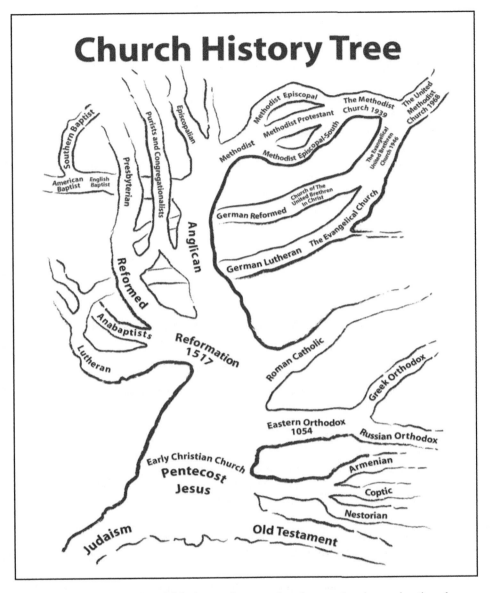

grown up in the Christian faith (many have not) to locate the denominational branch on which they were baptized or confirmed.

The family tree provides the opportunity for us to affirm that the body of Christ is larger than our branch of it and to claim what *The Book of Discipline of The United Methodist Church* calls "Our Common Heritage as Christians."[11]

With all Christians, we believe in the triune God—Father, Son, and Holy Spirit—as revealed in Scripture and affirmed in the historic affirmations of the Christian faith. The most commonly used creed in United Methodist churches is the Apostles' Creed. It was used as a baptismal creed in the earliest days of the Christian church and was affirmed in its present form in the third century.

I believe in God the Father Almighty,
　　maker of heaven and earth;
And in Jesus Christ his only Son our Lord:
　　who was conceived by the Holy Spirit,
　　born of the Virgin Mary,
　　suffered under Pontius Pilate,
　　was crucified, dead, and buried;
　　the third day he rose from the dead;
　　he ascended into heaven,
　　　　and sitteth at the right hand of God the Father Almighty;
　　from thence he shall come to judge the quick and the dead.
I believe in the Holy Spirit,
　　the holy catholic* church,
　　the communion of saints,
　　the forgiveness of sins,
　　the resurrection of the body,
　　and the life everlasting. Amen. [12]
　*(The small c means "universal.")

Based on the historical affirmations, the *Discipline* names the following elements in our common heritage:

- Faith in salvation in and through Jesus Christ.
- The belief that "God's redemptive love is realized in human life by the activity of the Holy Spirit, both in personal experience and in the community of believers."[13]
- Our understanding that we are part of Christ's universal church as we become conformed to Christ.
- Our faith in "the reign of God as both a present and a future reality."[14]
- The authority of Scripture, justification by grace through faith, and "the realization that the church is in need of continual reformation and renewal."[15]

At the same time, the family tree identifies the particular branch out of which The United Methodist Church emerged, namely, the Anglican branch of the Protestant Reformation.

Naming our history answers some of the most frequently asked questions people bring to the Pastor's Coffee. These questions will be discussed in more detail as we move along in *A Disciple's Path.*

- Why do you baptize infants?
- Why do you celebrate Holy Communion so often (a common question of former Baptists) or so seldom (a common question of former Episcopalians, Lutherans, or Roman Catholics)?
- Why do Methodist preachers move around? How are they appointed?
- Do I need to be rebaptized to join your church?
- What are the major differences between The United Methodist Church and the church in which I grew up?

Our Wesleyan Understanding of Grace

While affirming the faith we share in common with all other Christians, we also affirm the unique emphasis the Wesleyan tradition places on the love and grace of God. The *Discipline* defines grace as "the undeserved, unmerited, and loving action of God in human existence through the ever-present Holy Spirit . . . [which] precedes salvation as 'prevenient grace,' continues in 'justifying grace,' and is brought to fruition in 'sanctifying grace.'"[16] Because the Wesleyan understanding of grace provides the framework of *A Disciple's Path,* we will explore these ways of grace more deeply throughout our study.

Our Sacramental Life

As priests in the Church of England, the Wesleys stood in the spiritual tradition of the sixteenth-century Anglican theologian Richard Hooker, who defined a *sacrament* as "an outward and visible sign of an inward and spiritual grace."[17] Along with other Protestant churches, The United Methodist Church affirms two sacraments: baptism and Holy Communion, which is also known as the Lord's Supper or Eucharist. One distinguishing mark of the Oxford Methodists was their consistent presence in the Communion services in the university chapels. In his sermon "The Duty of Constant Communion," John Wesley declared, "It is the duty of every Christian to receive the Lord's Supper as often as he can."[18]

With amazing regularity, our Pastor's Coffee includes someone who comes from a Baptist background and someone who comes as a Roman Catholic. I often point them out as representing two poles of Christian understanding of the sacraments.

The Baptist pole tends to be more subjective. While affirming God's role in the sacrament, it focuses on our human response. In baptism individuals affirm that they have accepted God's grace and have claimed Jesus Christ as Lord, which is why Baptists do not baptize infants. In Communion, they remember what Jesus did at the Last Supper.

At the other pole, the Roman Catholic perspective is more objective. The emphasis is on what God is doing rather than on our response. What matters in baptism is God's action, though our response is included. In the Eucharist, the focus is on God's saving action in the bread and cup.

Influenced by our roots in the Anglican tradition, United Methodists are in the middle, tilting in the direction of the Roman Catholics. The primary emphasis is on what God is doing in the sacraments. They are means by which the intangible reality of God's grace touches our lives in tangible ways, through water, bread, and wine. But we also believe that our response really matters as by faith we receive the water of baptism, and the bread and cup of Communion with faith in Christ.

Baptism by sprinkling, pouring, or immersion is the sign of the grace of God that claims us as God's own children. It is the sacrament of initiation by which we are incorporated into the body of Christ, the beginning point of our spiritual journey. It is also the act in which baptized disciples are invited to remember our baptism and be grateful, not in the sense of remembering an event in the past, but in the sense of remembering who we are as people marked as Christian disciples in the waters of baptism. For these reasons baptism is celebrated in worship with congregational participation.

Holy Communion celebrates the grace of God that is present with us as we share in the body (the bread) and the blood (grape juice) of Christ. We do not believe that the elements actually become the body and blood of Christ, but that in them we experience the presence of the living Christ with us. In The United Methodist Church the table is open to all who come with faith in Christ regardless of their membership in any church.

As Anglican priests, the Wesley brothers placed great importance on the Holy Communion. Charles Wesley expressed it in one of his many Communion hymns:

> *Come and partake the gospel feast,*
> *be saved from sin, in Jesus rest;*
> *O taste the goodness of our God,*
> *and eat his flesh and drink his blood.*
> *See him set forth before your eyes;*
> *behold the bleeding sacrifice;*
> *his offered love make haste to embrace,*
> *and freely now be saved by grace.*[19]

For more information on the United Methodist understanding of the sacraments, I recommend *United Methodists and the Sacraments* by Gayle C. Felton (Nashville: Abingdon Press, 2007) or the pages on baptism and Communion at www.umc.org (search for "Sacraments & Faithful Living").

Our United Methodist Connection

As the Wesleyan Revival swept across eighteenth-century England, Wesley organized his preachers in what he referred to as the "connexion." It became the "Conference" that bound Wesley's leaders in England together and that sustained the circuit-riding preachers in frontier America.

Conferences have changed across the years. They now include laity as well as clergy and are much more democratic than they were in Wesley's day. But they are still the unique core of our life together as United Methodists.

The *Discipline* defines our connectional form of organization as "a vital web of interactive relationships."[20] It means that none of us are in ministry alone. Every United Methodist congregation is connected with every other United Methodist congregation around the world. That connection impacts everything from the way pastors are appointed to the way we fulfill our mission around the globe.

For more information on our connectional organization, go to "Our Church" at www.umc.org or *The Book of Discipline of The United Methodist Church.*

Our Mission

The mission of The United Methodist Church is "to make disciples of Jesus Christ for the transformation of the world."[21] It is our response to Jesus' final command to his first disciples: "Go therefore and make disciples of all nations, baptizing them in the name of the Father and of the Son and of the Holy Spirit, and teaching them to obey everything that I have commanded you" (Matthew 28:19-20).

The *Discipline* goes on to state that "local churches provide the most significant arena through which disciple-making occurs."[22] *A Disciple's Path* is designed to help every congregation fulfill that mission.

CHAPTER 1

Discipleship in the Way of Grace
A Disciple's Path Defined

Do you remember Alice's conversation with the Cheshire Cat during her journey through Wonderland? When she came to a fork in the road, she asked, "Would you tell me, please, which way I ought to go from here?" The Cat replied, "That depends a good deal on where you want to get to." She said, "I don't much care where." The Cat replied, "Then it doesn't matter which way you go."[1]

When we know where we are going, it makes a big difference how we get there. Like Jesus' first disciples, we've heard our Lord say, "Follow me!" Like them, we want to follow. But if we tell the truth, we often feel like Thomas, who said, "Lord, we do not know where you are going. How can we know the way?" (John 14:5-6). We want to know . . .

- Where is this path taking us?
- What's our destination?
- How will we get from where we are to where we want to be?

Jesus marked the destination of discipleship on the map of our souls in an intriguing conversation with a teacher of the law.

> "Teacher," he said, "what must I do to inherit eternal life?" [Jesus] said to him, "What is written in the law? What do you read there?" He answered, "You shall love the Lord your God with all your heart, and with all your soul, and with all your strength, and with all your mind; and your neighbor as yourself." And he said to him, "You have given the right answer; do this, and you will live." (Luke 10:25-28)

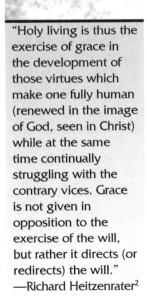

"Holy living is thus the exercise of grace in the development of those virtues which make one fully human (renewed in the image of God, seen in Christ) while at the same time continually struggling with the contrary vices. Grace is not given in opposition to the exercise of the will, but rather it directs (or redirects) the will."
—Richard Heitzenrater[2]

The destination of every disciple's path is a life that is completely centered in loving God and loving others, a life in which the love of God that became flesh in Jesus becomes flesh in us.

In 1734, a twenty-one-year-old Oxford student named Benjamin Ingham asked similar questions of John Wesley. Ingham's goal was a holy life. He knew that reaching that destination was not a directionless jaunt through the nondescript countryside of indistinct spirituality. He knew that being a disciple is more than drifting aimlessly from one spiritual high to another. He wanted to know the path that would lead toward the destination of a Christ-centered life.

Later in his ministry, John Wesley would use the term *Christian perfection* to mark the destination of a life that is completely aligned with the love of God. He wrote, "In a Christian believer *love* sits upon the throne which is erected in the inmost soul; namely, love of God and man, which fills the whole heart, and reigns without a rival."[3]

So, what does a disciple look like in the Wesleyan tradition? After a long time of searching and study, our team settled on this definition:

> A disciple is
> a follower of Jesus
> whose life is centering
> on loving God and loving others.

We chose the word *centering* instead of *centered* to indicate that discipleship is a lifelong experience of continuing transformation by the grace of God. It's what Friedrich Nietzsche called "a long obedience in the same direction."[4] The grace of God is instrumental in the process.

A Journey of Amazing Grace

"Amazing Grace," one of our best-loved hymns, includes these words: "'Tis grace hath brought me safe thus far, / and grace will lead me home."[5] John Newton (1725–1807), the former slave trader who penned that hymn, was influenced in his understanding of grace by his relationship with George Whitefield and John Wesley.

Wesley scholar Kenneth J. Collins has named the grace of God as "the key theme" of Wesley's theology. He writes, "There is no point in Wesley's theology of salvation where divine grace is not the leading motif."[6]

For Christian disciples in the Methodist tradition, the pathway of discipleship is an excellent adventure of amazing grace from beginning to end. Here's my homegrown definition of *grace:*

> Grace is the undeserved, unearned, unrepayable gift of the God who loves us enough to meet us where we are, but loves us too much to leave us there. Grace is the love of God at work within us to transform each of our lives into a unique expression of the love of God revealed in Jesus Christ, so that we become participants in God's transformation of the world.

As United Methodists, we often talk of three kinds or aspects of God's grace: prevenient, justifying, and sanctifying grace. Let's consider each one.

Prevenient Grace: The Love That Goes Before

John Wesley used the term *prevenient* grace—preventing or preparing grace—to describe the love of God that is active in our lives prior to our response. Prevenient grace is the love of God that seeks us before we seek God.

- It's the creative love that searched for Adam and Eve when, in their rebellion and sin, they tried to hide in the garden.
- It's the undeserved love of the God who "proves his love for us in that while we still were sinners, Christ died for us" (Romans 5:8).
- It's the unearned love that left John saying, "In this is love, not that we loved God but that he loved us. . . . We love because he first loved us" (1 John 4:10, 19).
- It's the seeking love that Jesus described as a shepherd who searches for one lost sheep or a woman who turns her house inside out looking for one lost coin.
- It's the pursuing love that Francis Thompson described as "The Hound of Heaven" who relentlessly hunted him day in and day out through the labyrinth of his own attempts to run from God until, finally, he fell before God and heard the Hound of Heaven say,

> *Ah, fondest, blindest, weakest,*
> *I am He Whom thou seekest!*[7]

Wesley defined *prevenient grace* as "the first wish to please God,—the first dawn of life concerning his will . . . the beginning of a deliverance from a blind, unfeeling heart, quite insensible of God."[8] It's the love we did nothing to deserve, the love that prepares us to experience God's forgiveness. But we have a hard time comprehending it because we like to think that we can find God.

Some years ago a Christian organization launched a nationwide evangelistic campaign with the theme "I Found It." It was a simple way of saying, "I have found new life in Christ and I want you to find it too." But there's a biblical problem with that slogan.

The Bible is not the story of the way we find God; it's the story of the way God comes seeking us. We are the ones who are lost, the ones who hide from the naked truth about ourselves. We get disoriented in the chaos and confusion of the world. We lose our way in our radical self-absorption and squander our souls in meaningless living. God is the one who comes to find us. That's prevenient grace.

United Methodists affirm prevenient grace in the sacrament of infant baptism. When someone asks what good baptism does when the child isn't aware of what's

> Stupendous love of God most high!
> He comes to meet us from the sky
> in mildest majesty;
> full of unutterable grace,
> He calls the weary burdened race,
> "Come all for help to me."
> —Charles Wesley[9]

happening, I say that's just the point. Long before we were aware of it, long before we responded in commitment to Christ, God already loved us, searched for us, tracked us down. While we were still sinners, Christ died for us. Any love we have for God is because God loved us first (see 1 John 4:7-12). That's prevenient grace.

In Arthur Miller's classic play *Death of a Salesman*, Willy Loman's life is consumed by the fantasy that if he could make one big deal, he might be loved and accepted by his son, Biff. Toward the end of the play, it suddenly hits Willy that his son might just love him after all. Willy looks up in awestricken amazement and says, "Isn't that—isn't that remarkable? Biff—he likes me!" Willy's wife replies, "He loves you, Willy!" Biff's younger brother adds, "Always did, Pop."[10]

Somewhere along the way, we discover that God loved us before we loved God, always loved us and always will. That's prevenient grace. An unknown hymn writer who experienced God's prevenient grace wrote,

> *I sought the Lord, and afterward I knew*
> *He moved my soul to seek him, seeking me;*
> *It was not I that found, O Savior true;*
> *No, I was found of thee.*[11]

Justifying Grace: The Love that Makes Things Right

Prevenient grace leads us to what Wesley called *justifying* grace. So, what does it mean to be justified?

If you look at the tool bar on most computer screens, you'll find an icon that will "justify" the type to fit evenly within the margins on both sides of the screen. To justify is to realign the words and letters in each line so that they are in right relationship with each other and with the page on which they appear.

That's not far from what the Apostle Paul was talking about when he wrote, "Since we are justified by faith, we have peace with God through our Lord Jesus Christ, through whom we have obtained access to this grace in which we stand" (Romans 5:1-2). Justification is God's love in Christ that brings us into right relationship with God and with one another. It's the way God makes things right.

But how do things get out of line in the first place?

Paul opens his letter to the Romans with a graphic description of human life that is out of line with what God intends. The Bible calls it "sin." Not "sins" plural, which are like individual letters on the screen, but "sin" singular, as the overall condition of human life that is out of alignment with the life-giving purpose of God.

The Bible goes on to say that sin is not solely our own, private business, like saying that it doesn't matter what we do as long as it doesn't hurt someone else. Human life is more interconnected than that. English poet John Donne said that "no man is an island, entire of itself."[12] We are all part of the main. My "sins" are like individual letters that disrupt the alignment of the entire page. One letter out of place displaces all the others.

But things get worse. The Bible says there is an aggressive quality to sin. Sin is like cancer cells that rebel against God's life-giving purpose and becomes life destroying. Sin is active rebellion against the loving God who is relentlessly at work to heal, restore, and make things right.

And here's the worst part of all. We're all infected with it. Paul says, "You have no excuse, whoever you are. . . . For there is no distinction, since all have sinned and fall short of the glory of God" (Romans 2:1; 3:22-23). That's sin.

But we don't like to admit that we are involved in the sin business. We're such nice, polite, well-bred, socially acceptable folks that we have a hard time thinking of ourselves as sinners. Like Adam and Eve trying to hide their nakedness in the garden, we like to pretend that our lives are neatly in line and everything is under control.

But hold on a minute. Do you remember our destination?

- Have we arrived at a life that is fully centered in Christ?
- Is every inch of type in our lives in perfect alignment with God's love?
- Do we love God with our whole hearts, souls, minds, and strength? No reservations, no compromises, no hidden selfish agendas?
- Do we love others the way we love ourselves, much less the way we have been loved by God?

If we tell the truth, there's ample evidence that we have all fallen short of the full glory of God. That's sin.

But here's the good news!

Since we are justified by faith, we have peace with God through our Lord Jesus Christ, through whom we have obtained access to this grace in which we stand. . . . God proves his love for us in that while we still were sinners Christ died for us. . . . For if while we were enemies, we were reconciled to God through the death of his Son, much more surely, having been reconciled, will we be saved by his life. . . . Where sin increased, grace abounded all the more, so that, just as sin exercised dominion in death, so grace might also exercise dominion through justification leading to eternal life through Jesus Christ our Lord. (Romans 5:1, 8, 10, 20-21)

"By sin, I here understand inward sin; any sinful temper, passion, or affection; such as pride, self-will, love of the world, in any kind or degree; such as lust, anger, peevishness; any disposition contrary to the mind which was in Christ."

—John Wesley[13]

The almost unbelievable good news is that God, in an act of unearned, extravagant grace, meets us in the middle of the mess we've made of things and, by the self-giving love of Jesus on the cross, restores us to right relationship with himself. The cross is the place where God makes things right. That is God's justifying grace.

The word we use to describe what happened when we experience this grace is *conversion*. The *Discipline* affirms that conversion "may be sudden and dramatic, or gradual and cumulative. It marks a new beginning, yet it is part of an ongoing process. . . . [It] always expresses itself as faith working by love."[14] E. Stanley Jones, the great missionary leader of Methodism in the twentieth century, simply said, "Conversion is conversion from a self-centered person to a God-centered person."[15]

And here's the kicker. There's nothing we can do to earn or deserve it. It is the pure, unadulterated gift of God's grace. All we need to do is to acknowledge our need, receive it as a gift, and align our living with it. Charles Wesley's hymns reverberate with amazement at the love and grace of God with lines like this: "Amazing love! How can it be that thou, my God, shouldst die for me?"[16]

Jesus made the point when he said that a Pharisee and a tax collector went up to the temple to pray. We immediately know which one was the good guy. The Pharisee. He was an upstanding, churchgoing, law-abiding, decent person, like most of us. The bad guy was the tax collector—corrupt, dishonest, and crooked as the day is long.

Jesus said the Pharisee was "standing by himself" when he said, "God, I thank you that I am not like other people: thieves, rogues, adulterers, or even like this tax collector" (Luke 18:11). By contrast, the tax collector "would not even look up to heaven, but was beating his breast and saying, 'God, be merciful to me, a sinner!'" (Luke 18:13). Here's the punch line to the story. Jesus said of the tax collector, "I tell you, this man went down to his home justified rather than the other" (Luke 18:14).

The invitation to each of us is to acknowledge just how much we need to be justified and to receive the grace that only God can give.

Sanctifying Grace: The Love That Just Won't Quit

We have seen that God's love goes before us (prevenient grace) and that God's love makes things right (justifying grace). God's love also never quits. This is what we call *sanctifying* grace—grace that sustains us and perfects us in love.

Here's a question that can make competent clergy stop in their tracks, wrinkle their eyebrows, and take a deep gulp before they answer it. It has been asked of every preacher who has been ordained in the Methodist ministry since Wesley first asked it of his traveling preachers: "Are you going on to perfection?"

"From the time of our being born again, the gradual work of sanctification takes place. . . . We are more and more alive to God. We go on from grace to grace."
—John Wesley[17]

One response might be, "You've got to be kidding! Nobody's perfect!" Wesley would agree that's absolutely true. Not one of us has reached flawless perfection. To say that we have simply proves that we haven't. The gospel is clear that Jesus will take a humble sinner over a self-righteous saint any day.

24

But the question is: Are you *going on* to perfection? It's a question that goes to the heart of our understanding of grace, a question that never stops leading us in the direction of a more Christ-centered life.

The destination of the discipleship pathway is a life that is perfectly centered in and controlled by the love of God in Christ. Wesley called the destination "Christian perfection" or "being made perfect in love."

The Apostle Paul relies on directional language to describe the Christian life by using a very strong Greek verb:

> Those who live according to the flesh *set their minds* on the things of the flesh, but those who live according to the Spirit *set their minds* on the things of the Spirit. To *set the mind* on the flesh is death, but to *set the mind* on the Spirit is life and peace. (Romans 8:5-6, emphasis added)

The Gospel writer uses the same phrase to say that Jesus "set his face to go to Jerusalem" (Luke 9:51 KJV), where he knew he would face the cross.

Christian perfection, the process of being made perfect in love, is about setting our minds in the direction of a life that is perfectly, completely, fully centered in the love of God in Christ.

So, the question becomes:

- Why would we settle for anything less than that kind of perfection?
- Why would we stop somewhere along the way and miss our final destination?
- If we aren't going on to perfection, then where do we think we are going?

Another response to Wesley's question would be to say that the road to perfection is paved with grace. Sanctifying grace is the love that continues to shape our lives into the likeness of Jesus Christ all along the way. Sanctifying grace is the love that leads us on. It's the love that never quits.

A farmer in the little church that I served in north central Florida didn't have much formal education, but he had a lot of common sense. One day I asked, "How are you doing?" He said, "Well, Preacher, I'm not the man I used to be, and I'm not yet the man I hope to be, but I'm more the man I'd like to be than I've ever been before."

Remember that. That's about as good a description of sanctification as I've ever heard. That guy knew where he had been. He knew where he was. And he knew the direction in which he was going. It's the kind of perfection that is made possible within us by the grace of the God who loves us enough to meet us where we are, but loves us too much to leave us there. It's the sanctifying grace that leads us on. In one of my favorite hymns by Charles Wesley we sing:

> *Finish, then, thy new creation;*
> *pure and spotless let us be.*
> *Let us see thy great salvation*

perfectly restored in thee;
changed from glory into glory,
till in heaven we take our place,
till we cast our crowns before thee,
lost in wonder, love, and praise.[18]

Are you going on to perfection? Wesley followed that question with two more questions.

"Do you expect to be made perfect in love in this life?" In other words, do you expect God's grace to make a tangible difference in the way you live right now? Do you really believe that your life, right here, right now, can become a life that is more deeply centered in loving God and loving others? Do you expect to become a more loving, more Christlike person tomorrow than you are today?

Wesley's second question was this: "Are you earnestly seeking after it?" It's one thing to mark the destination on the map, but it's quite another to keep moving toward it. It's one thing to say that we would like to be a Christ-centered person, but it's something else to practice the spiritual disciplines that will take us there.

As United Methodists, we affirm the time-tested practices of discipleship when we commit our prayers, presence, gifts, service, and witness. In the weeks ahead, we'll look more closely at those practices as we journey along the way of grace that leads to a life that is centered in Jesus Christ.

"The empowering grace of God is already present, even before we are fully aware of its presence. More important, perhaps, this grace ever invites response. The grace of God ever meets us at our present level and then beckons us to go further."
—Kenneth J. Collins[19]

Chapter 2

The Path of Biblical Prayer
Prayer and Scripture Meditation

I came across a shocking statistic in the book *Immunity to Change.* Cardiologists report that only one in seven patients makes the lifestyle changes—stop smoking, lose weight, eat right, get exercise—that could save their lives.[1]

One in seven! If those are the odds cardiologists face in convincing heart patients to change their behavior, what kinds of odds do we face as disciples of Jesus Christ? We are, after all, called to live transformed lives; lives that are not conformed to the assumptions and values of the world around us, but lives that are "transformed by the renewing of [our] minds"; lives that are fully aligned with the will of God revealed in Jesus Christ (see Romans 12:2). And we're not just talking about external changes in outward behaviors. We're talking about radical, pervasive change that goes all the way to the heart.

Jesus taught that the greatest commandment is to love God with all our hearts, souls, minds, and strength, followed by the commandment that we love our neighbor as we love ourselves. John Wesley followed Jesus' teaching and placed these two commandments at the center of the Christian life. He defined "true religion" as "a heart right toward God and man." He taught that it "does not consist . . . in any outward thing whatever, in anything exterior to the heart." He was convinced that we can be orthodox in our beliefs and correct in our behavior, but we might still be "a stranger . . . to the religion of the heart."[2]

> "Although true religion naturally leads to every good word and work, yet the real nature thereof lies deeper still, even in 'the hidden man of the heart.'"
> —John Wesley[3]

In the Methodist tradition, the heart of the matter is always a matter of the heart. The pathway of discipleship involves a change in belief and action that results in the transformation of our hearts.

In 1730, John and Charles Wesley began meeting with a few Oxford friends with the sole intention of helping each other live holy lives. They met regularly to study the Scripture, to pray together, and to engage in what they called "religious talk." No one paid attention to them until they began showing up with unusual regularity for Holy Communion at Christ Church, visiting the prisons, and serving the poor. These public acts of worship and service brought upon them the name "Holy Club."

In 1732, they began practicing spiritual disciplines that were modeled after the practices of the early church. Because they were so intensely methodical in these disciplines, they were mockingly called "Methodists," and the name has been with us ever since.[4] Their lifestyle changes resulted in the transformation of their hearts.

Wherever we are in our spiritual journey, as disciples of Jesus Christ in The United Methodist Church, we are called to break through our immunity to change by practicing the spiritual disciplines that lead toward a life centered in the love of God in Christ so that we can participate in God's transformation of the world.

Practicing Prayer

It's appropriate that in our membership vows, the first practice to which we commit ourselves is prayer. John Wesley's first published work was *A Collection of Forms of Prayer for Every Day in the Week* (1733). Along with prayers, it contained questions for self-examination focused on the virtues of a holy life. Benjamin Ingham's diary records that he was meeting with Charles Wesley when he began using John Wesley's book as a guide for his practice of prayer.[5] On the opening pages of his diary, Ingham transcribed Thomas Ken's "Collect for Every Hour" and the Anglican "Collect for Purity":

"Wesley knew that a life of prayer was not an accident or a natural consequence of just living. He was convinced that a life of prayer was the result of a determined and disciplined effort . . . without this disciplined effort, prayer would become secondary and our relationship with God left to suffocate under the cares and delights of the world."

—Rueben Job[7]

Almighty God, unto Whom all hearts be open, all desires known, and from Whom no secrets are hid: Cleanse the thoughts of our hearts by the inspiration of Thy Holy Spirit, that we may perfectly love Thee, and worthily magnify Thy holy Name: through Christ our Lord. Amen.[6]

Every page of Ingham's diary bears witness to the central role of personal and public prayer in the lives of the first Methodists at Oxford, an emphasis that remained at the center of the Wesleyan movement. But let's be truthful. We United Methodists still say we believe in prayer; the question is whether we believe that praying makes any real difference and whether we have learned the methods that will help us experience it.

I'll confess that I've been to more church meetings than I can count that opened and closed with prayer, yet nothing that happened between the two prayers gave any evidence that we thought the praying made any difference.

I heard about a congregation of teetotaling Methodists who prayed for years that the Lord would do something about the disreputable bar across the street from the church. One night the bar was hit by lightning and burned to the ground. The bar owner promptly sued the church, saying that the congregation's prayers were responsible for the fire. The church contested the suit. After hearing the case, the judge said, "I'm not sure how I'll rule on this case, but one thing is clear. The bar owner believes in prayer, and the church people don't."

So, what are the odds that you or your church might be sued because of the effectiveness of your prayers? How might we practice prayer in a way that will make a tangible difference in the way we live?

Let's begin by clearing the deck of the idea that prayer is a magic trick by which we manipulate God's power to get what we want done. In Scripture, the primary purpose of prayer is to enable us to live in an intimate relationship with God so that we become the agents of God's saving purpose in this world. Prayer is not the process by which we get what we want from God, but the relationship in which God gets what God wants in and through us. Wesley expressed this understanding in his Covenant Prayer, which says, "I am no longer my own, but thine. . . . Let me be employed for thee or laid aside for thee, exalted for thee or brought low for thee."[8]

Like every human relationship, the dynamics of our relationship with God change as we grow, but four essential building blocks in that relationship are expressed in the acronym ACTS.

Adoration
Confession
Thanksgiving
Supplication

The biblical story of Ezra and Nehemiah, who were instrumental in rebuilding the temple in Jerusalem after the Babylonian exile, provides a model for the way those building blocks can be at work in our lives. Let's consider four building blocks of a life of prayer.

1. Adoration

Prayer begins not with who we are or what we want from God but with who God is and what God wants for us. Adoration is the way we remind ourselves of the character of the God to whom we pray. That's where Nehemiah began when he prayed: "O LORD God of heaven, the great and awesome God who keeps covenant and steadfast love with those who love him and keep his commandments" (Nehemiah 1:5).

Ezra expressed the same spirit of adoration when he prayed:

> You are the LORD, you alone; you have made heaven, the heaven of
> heavens, with all their host, the earth and all that is on it, the seas and
> all that is in them. To all of them you give life, and the host of heaven

worships you. . . . You are a God ready to forgive, gracious and merciful, slow to anger and abounding in steadfast love. (Nehemiah 9:6, 17)

Adoration is where Jesus began when he taught his disciples to pray, "Our Father in heaven, hallowed be your name." It's the way many of us uttered our earliest childhood prayer, "God is great; God is good."

The character of the God to whom we pray makes a difference in the way we pray and the way we live. It's not enough for God to be great unless God is also good. An awesome god can be an awful god unless God is awesome in being— like a loving parent who is ready to forgive, gracious and merciful, abounding in steadfast love.

2. Confession

Nehemiah expressed his confession with tears:

> When I heard these words I sat down and wept, and mourned for days.
> . . . Let your ear be attentive and your eyes open to hear the prayer of
> your servant that I now pray before you day and night for your servants,
> the people of Israel, confessing the sins of the people of Israel, which
> we have sinned against you. (Nehemiah 1:4-6)

In the same way, Ezra acknowledged the persistent faithfulness of his people while claiming the love and forgiveness of God: "Our ancestors acted presumptuously and stiffened their necks and did not obey your commandments. . . . But you are a God ready to forgive, gracious and merciful, slow to anger and abounding in steadfast love, and you did not forsake them" (Nehemiah 9:16-17).

Confession is the way we face the hard truth about who we are and where we are in our discipleship. Confession is the way we name the stuff that clutters our souls and gets in the way of a vibrant relationship with God. It's the way we acknowledge that we are not as perfect as we pretend, not as good as we would like, and not as loving as our dog or cat may think we are. The folks in Alcoholics Anonymous call it a "searching and fearless moral inventory."[9]

The Oxford Methodists were intensely methodical in self-examination. Here are a few of the questions Benjamin Ingham received from Charles Wesley and asked himself every day:

- Have I prayed with fervor by myself and at Church?
- Have I said or done anything without a present or previous perception of its remote or immediate tendency to the glory of God?
- Have I after every pleasure immediately given thanks?
- Have I been zealous in undertaking, and active in doing what good I could?

- Have I been or seemed angry?
- Have I thought or spoke unkindly of or to anyone?[10]

Confession would be the only appropriate response to questions like those! Confession is the recognition of our constant need of God's forgiveness and grace.

3. Thanksgiving

Nehemiah captured the spirit of thanksgiving in his description of the dedication of the rebuilt wall of the temple:

> Now at the dedication of the wall of Jerusalem they sought out the Levites in all their places, to bring them to Jerusalem to celebrate the dedication with rejoicing, with thanksgivings and with singing, with cymbals, harps, and lyres. . . . The joy of Jerusalem was heard far away. (Nehemiah 12:27, 43)

That's what I call thanksgiving! With or without cymbals, it is our joyful response to the way God is at work for good in our lives and the world around us.

On Easter Day, 1734, Benjamin Ingham recorded a set of resolutions by which he determined to "make an entire surrender" of himself to God. It included a renewal of his baptismal vows and confirmed his commitment while receiving the Holy Communion at the altar of Queen's College Chapel. His resolutions concluded with a prayer of praise in which he gave thanks for all of God's grace in his life to the glory of the Trinity.[11]

Try it sometime. Instead of listing all the anxieties, burdens, frustrations, and failures of your life, begin with the words: "Thank you, Lord for . . . " and fill in the blanks. In times when we are surrounded by cynicism, fear, anger, and just plain meanness, it can make a huge difference to be grounded in a joyful spirit of thanksgiving.

4. Supplication

Nehemiah turned to God in supplication when he prayed: "O Lord, let your ear be attentive to the prayer of your servant, and to the prayer of your servants who delight in revering your name. Give success to your servant today, and grant him mercy in the sight of this man!" (Nehemiah 1:11).

Another word for supplication is *intercession*. Intercession is more than lifting up a shopping list of prayer requests and asking God to do something about them. Intercession is the way we draw the very real concerns of our lives and our world into the presence of God and invite God to be at work in them through us.

Steve Harper pointed out that John Wesley's *Journal* reveals "the full range of prayer. He praised, confessed, gave thanks, interceded for others, and let his own

Pray without ceasing, pray,
(your Captain gives the word)
his summons cheerfully obey
and call upon the Lord;
to God your every want
in instant prayer display,
pray always, pray and never
faint,
pray, without ceasing pray.
　　　　—Charles Wesley[13]

requests be made known unto God. . . . Often Wesley bared his soul before God in doubts, questions, and even cries of anguish."[12]

The problem with a lot of what passes for prayer is that we begin where we should end. We begin with supplication or intercession as we bring a long list of concerns to God, and then we wonder why nothing seems to happen. The ACTS pattern turns things the other way around by beginning with adoration, the awareness of who God is, which leads to confession, in which we clear the deck of all the stuff that gets in the way of God's spirit at work in our lives. Having experienced God's forgiveness, we respond with thanksgiving. Then, and perhaps only then, are we prepared to bring into God's presence all the real, messy, painful stuff of our lives and of our world. But it's the kind of praying that has the power to change our hearts.

There is, however, a critical issue we need to confront in developing a discipline of prayer. Not every kind of praying will carry us along the path that leads from a self-centered life to a life that is centered in Jesus Christ. Not every expression of spirituality will enable us to love God and love others. Not every form of religious practice will energize us to share in God's transformation of the world. If our destination is a life that is centering in Jesus Christ so that we can participate in God's transformation of the world, our life of prayer must be shaped by disciplined reflection on Scripture.

People of the Book

The *Discipline* affirms that one of the beliefs we hold in common with other Christians is "the authority of Scripture in matters of faith."[14] This affirmation grounds us in the long history of Christian tradition, reaching back to the earliest days of the faith when the Apostle Paul instructed his young protégé, Timothy, to "continue in what you have learned and firmly believed, knowing from whom you learned it, and how from childhood you have known the sacred writings that are able to instruct you for salvation through faith in Christ Jesus" (2 Timothy 3:14-15).

In 1784, John Wesley revised the Articles of Religion of the Church of England and sent them to America for the newly formed Methodist Episcopal Church, thereby planting the roots of the Methodist movement in America in the line of the Protestant Reformation. Article V declares that Holy Scripture contains "all things necessary to salvation." It goes on to say that anything that is not contained in or proved by Scripture cannot be required for salvation.[15] The history of our faith is a clear affirmation of the importance of Scripture in our continued growth as disciples of Jesus Christ.

John Wesley called himself "a man of one book."[16] The Latin phrase *homo unius libri* originated with Thomas Aquinas (1225–1274) and demonstrated Wesley's saturation in the writings of the early church fathers. Wesley applied that term not only to himself, but also to each of the Oxford Methodists.

It's wasn't literally true. Wesley was one of the best-read and most widely published Christians of his era. When Benjamin Ingham asked for a method for his spiritual growth, Wesley gave him a list of classic writers of Christian devotion for use in his small group.

He was, however, a "man of one book" in that nothing took priority over reading Scripture. In his *Complete English Dictionary* (1753), Wesley defined a *Methodist* as "one that lives according to the method laid down in the Bible."[17] He instructed Ingham to test everything he read or did by what he found in Scripture. Wesley knew that we can be "spiritual" without the Bible, but we can never be growing disciples of Jesus Christ without disciplined study of and reflection on the written word.

> "I want to know one thing, the way to heaven. . . . God Himself has condescended to teach me the way. . . . He has written it down in a book. O give me that book! At any price, give me the book of God! I have it: here is knowledge enough for me. Let me be *homo unius libri* (a man of one book)."
> —John Wesley[18]

Throughout my years in ministry I've been asked several basic questions from people who are moving into disciplined reflection on Scripture. Though clearly not complete, my initial responses to those questions may be a starting point for your own exploration of Scripture within the Wesleyan tradition.

• Question #1: Is the Bible true?

It's easy enough to answer yes. But the question behind the question is: *How is* the Bible true? *What* is it true about?

We've been conditioned by the Enlightenment, the modern era, and the scientific method to assume that the only things that are true are things that can be proved on the basis of scientific data and empirical evidence. That is, of course, one kind of truth.

But there are other kinds of truth. Those who have experienced Shakespeare's *King Lear* know that you don't need a birth certificate for a baby named Lear to know that the play is true in ways that go beyond the limitations of empirical evidence. It's true to the deepest, most painful realities of the human life and soul.

The Bible contains both kinds of truth. It is rooted in historically verifiable events, but its truth goes beyond anything that can be proved by the scientific method. It's true in the way it claims to be true, namely, in telling us the story of God's relationship with God's creation. It touches the deepest truth of your life and mine, revealing the truth about who God is and what God intends for us.

• Question #2: Is the Bible inspired?

Paul declared that "all scripture is inspired" (2 Timothy 3:16). But what does *inspired* mean?

The Greek word for inspired means "God-breathed." It's reminiscent of the way Genesis says that the Spirit—literally, the "breath" or "wind" of God—breathed life into the human being and Adam became a living soul. It's similar to what we mean when we say that artists or musicians were inspired when they created their works of art. When we see the paintings or hear the music, we experience the same inspiration.

For most biblical scholars throughout Christian history, *inspired* does not mean that God dictated every word to passive secretaries who wrote it down just the way it appears in the King James translation, with the words of Jesus in red-letter print.

Inspired means that something happened; God acted. Real human beings in real time and space experienced God's presence in a real and personal way. They told their story. That story was told and retold by the community of faith. Then, fairly recently, it was written down and passed on to us. When we read the story, we can experience the same spirit of God, breathing life into the written word so that it becomes a living Word in us.

• Question #3: Should we take the Bible literally or figuratively?

My answer is that we need to take it seriously. That means taking seriously the context in which each book was written and the rich variety of literary forms in which it comes to us.

I often say that I read the Bible the way I read the Sunday edition of the *New York Times*.

Sometimes it reads like the front-page account of an actual historical event.

Sometimes it's like reading the book reviews or arts section as it speaks through parable and poetry, story and song.

Sometimes it reads like the sports section when life feels like good and evil struggling to win a victory.

Sometimes Paul's letters are like reading the opinion pages, while reading the prophets is like reading movie previews filled with fantastic images and mind-blowing metaphors.

None of it reads like a scientific textbook or a self-help manual.

The grand sweep of the biblical story is the account of a life-changing experience with God that required the use of nearly every literary form to attempt to convey it.

When we take the Bible seriously in terms of the context in which it was written and the form in which it comes to us, we begin to discover what Paul meant when he said that Scripture is "useful for teaching, for reproof, for correction, and for training in righteousness, so that everyone who belongs to God may be . . . equipped for every good work" (2 Timothy 3:16-17). That's what the Bible is meant to do.

• Question #4: How do Christians in the Methodist tradition read, interpret, and apply Scripture to their lives?

John Wesley gave the early Methodists a way of interpreting Scripture that has come to be known as "the Wesleyan Quadrilateral," though he never used that term.

Scripture is the bottom line. It's the foundation upon which everything else depends. Like Wesley and the early Methodists, we are called to be "people of one book." The *Discipline* defines Scripture as "the primary source and criterion for Christian doctrine."[19]

There are three tools by which United Methodists interpret Scripture and apply it to their lives. One is **tradition.** It's the gathered wisdom of faithful Christians who have gone before us. We are accountable to the traditions of biblical study that have been passed down to us. At the same time, we are accountable to the specific part of Christian tradition in which we stand.

For example, all Christians practice the sacraments of baptism and Communion. But how we practice them is determined by the specific part of the Christian tradition in which we live. That's why the United Methodist practice of the sacraments is different from that of our Catholic brothers and sisters on one side and our Baptist brothers and sisters on the other. It's about tradition.

The second tool is **reason.** On her journey through Wonderland, Alice hears the White Queen say, "Sometimes I've believed as many as six impossible things before breakfast."[20] She wasn't a United Methodist! We believe that God expects us to use our brains and that the faith we experience in our hearts should make sense in our heads. It also means that we allow people the space they need to question, think, and grow.

Scripture, tradition, and reason were basic parts of the Anglican tradition to which Wesley added the third tool: **experience.** The *Discipline* states, "All religious experience affects all human experience; all human experience affects our understanding of religious experience."[21]

I remember an old-time Methodist preacher who said that an experience is the experience you experience when you experience an experience. Our human experiences and our experience of the spirit of God have a direct influence on the way we read and interpret Scripture.

Tradition, reason, and experience are the boundary lines within which United Methodists interpret Scripture and apply it in our lives. The result is that equally faithful United Methodists may read the same text and come to different conclusions about the way it speaks to our lives. By sharing our unique understanding of Scripture in community with others, the written word becomes a living Word in our lives.

In the preface to his *Explanatory Notes upon the Old Testament,* Wesley offered his advice for the effective reading of Scripture. Here is my paraphrase of his words:

- Set aside time every day for reflection on Scripture.
- Read with the single intention of knowing the will of God, and make your own resolution to follow it.
- Begin your time with prayer so that your understanding of Scripture is shaped by the Spirit who inspired it. Close your Scripture reading in prayer so that the words you read will be embedded in your heart.
- Pause to examine yourself by what you read in order to praise God for the ways your life has conformed to God's will and to be conscious of the ways in which you have fallen short.
- Use whatever insight you receive immediately so that the written word will have its full power in your life.[22]

As a whole, Benjamin Ingham's diary confirms that the daily, even hourly, practices of meditation, self-examination, prayer, and reflection on Scripture were the central disciplines by which the Oxford Methodists grew into what they called "the holy life."

In the twentieth century, Henri Nouwen stood well within the spiritual tradition of the Wesleys when he wrote that "discipleship cannot be realized without discipline." He pointed out that "the discipline of the Christian disciple is not to master anything, but rather to be mastered by the Spirit. True Christian discipline is the human effort to create the space in which the Spirit of Christ can transform us into his image."[23]

Prayer and Scripture are the nonnegotiable essentials for the journey of discipleship. Without them, we run out of steam or get sidetracked along the way. They are the practices by which we become faithful disciples whose lives are centering in Jesus Christ and through whom the love of God begins to transform the world.

CHAPTER 3

The Priority of Presence
Corporate Worship and Small-group Community

Cancer brought Larry to me. He had not had direct contact with the Christian faith for nearly three decades. But when he received the diagnosis, he began to wonder about where he could turn for spiritual support. He had noticed the way a fellow attorney lived her faith in a quiet, unassuming way. He had seen her leave the office to participate in her Disciple Bible Study group. He thought that if he ever was interested in finding a church, hers might be the place to begin.

He asked his question in total sincerity: "Can I get to know Jesus without being involved in the church?" It's the kind of question that many spiritually hungry folks are asking these days.

I replied that because I believe Christ is risen and present in this world, I suspect that it's possible to run into him just about anywhere and that he could get to know the story of Jesus by reading the Bible. But I also said that I know of no way to experience the fullness of Christ's presence without being a part of a Christian community in which to worship and grow as a disciple of Jesus Christ.

When he asked where to begin, I suggested that he read the Gospels and get to know Jesus the way he is described there. I recommended Henri Nouwen's book *Letters to Marc About Jesus*, and I gave him a copy of my book *Journey to the Center of the Faith*. I also invited him to try out a small group of men with whom I meet on Monday mornings.

Larry took the bait, and the Spirit did the rest. He was present in worship on Sunday, and to my surprise, he showed up for the men's group on Monday morning. He had already read the Gospels, and with the excitement of a new discovery, he said, "I like this Jesus. He's really cool."

As he began to grow, he asked, "Now, what's this I hear about baptism?" Members of our men's group were present in the worship service in which he was baptized. They surrounded him with prayer, e-mails, and friendship as he went through the surgery and chemotherapy. He described an amazing peace that filled his life as he went through the treatments. He has continued to grow and now helps lead that men's group in Bible study.

It's possible that Larry would have gotten to know Christ without the church, but I wouldn't want to bet on it. It mattered that he showed up. His presence made a difference.

"No one goes to heaven alone."
— Eugene Nicholas Heidt[1]

The Necessity of Community

Every page of Benjamin Ingham's diary records the names of fellow Oxford students who joined him in the disciplines by which they could develop a holy life. The names bear witness to a biblically nonnegotiable discipline for anyone who would follow Jesus in the pathway of discipleship. Let's call it the "priority of presence."

No one walks the discipleship pathway alone. There is no such thing as solitary Christianity. Being a follower of Jesus means being in community with other followers of Jesus. We can be religious or spiritual without the presence of other people in our lives, but we cannot be growing disciples of Jesus Christ without the encouragement, guidance, wisdom, and accountability of other disciples.

E. Stanley Jones was one of the missionary heroes of twentieth-century Methodism. He left an indelible mark on my understanding of the Christian life when, as a student in the college where Jones responded to God's call on his life, I heard him say that everyone who belongs to Christ belongs to everyone who belongs to Christ.[2]

More recently, Archbishop Desmond Tutu demonstrated the importance of the African concept of *ubuntu*, which he defined as meaning, "My humanity is caught up, is inextricably bound up, in yours. . . . A person is a person through other persons."[3] We find our humanity in our connections with others. A self-made individual is an oxymoron. I am who I am because you are who you are.

Jesus demonstrated life in community by calling twelve ordinary men to become his disciples. He promised that wherever two or three are gathered together, he would be among them. At the Last Supper, he raised Christian friendship to a sacramental level when he said, "I do not call you servants any longer . . . I have called you friends" (John 15:15). The Apostle Paul told the disciples in Corinth, "Now you are the body of Christ and individually members of it" (1 Corinthians 12:27).

Here's the way the writer of the epistle to the Hebrews reinforced the priority of presence:

> Let us hold fast to the confession of our hope without wavering, for he who has promised is faithful. And let us consider how to provoke one another to love and good deeds, not neglecting to meet together, as is the habit of some, but encouraging one another, and all the more as you see the Day approaching. (Hebrews 10:23-25)

My personal illustration of this principle involves my twin brother. My life is inextricably bound together with his. I did not choose him. He was given to me at birth. I've never known what it would mean to live without him in my life. In the same way, being "born again" by God's love in Christ means being born into a family with brothers and sisters who are given to me in God's love. My life as a disciple is inextricably bound together with other disciples of Jesus Christ.

The priority of presence—our presence in the lives of others and their presence in ours—runs directly against the grain of the pull-yourself-up-by-your-own-bootstraps mentality of our overly individualized American culture. But it is essential to a biblical understanding of discipleship, particularly in the Methodist tradition.

> "Directly opposite to this is the gospel of Christ. Solitary religion is not to be found there. 'Holy solitaries' is a phrase no more consistent with the gospel than holy adulterers. The gospel of Christ knows of no religion, but social; no holiness but social holiness."
>
> —John Wesley[5]

Methodists love to retell the story of John Wesley's heart-warming experience on May 24, 1738. He records in his *Journal* that he went "very unwillingly" to a small-group Bible study that was meeting in Aldersgate Street in London. He went unwillingly, but he went. He was present. That night, the spirit of God touched his heart. He wrote, "I felt my heart strangely warmed."[4] That heart-warming experience was a critically important stop along his personal journey of discipleship, which helped ignite the spiritual awakening that swept across England and became the Methodist movement around the world.

But what would have happened—or more to the point, what would *not* have happened—if Wesley had not been "unwillingly" present that night?

I cannot promise that our hearts will be "strangely warmed" every time we are present with a small group or present in worship with the gathered congregation. But I can promise that it won't happen if we aren't there. Our presence matters because it could result in the transformation of our lives.

The writer of the Hebrew letter challenges us to "hold fast to the confession of our hope without wavering" (Hebrews 10:23). That's not always an easy thing to do. In a world like this, it can be tough to hold on to hope. That's why the writer tells us to look for ways to "provoke one another to love and good deeds . . . encouraging one another" (Hebrews 10:24-25). Our presence with one another is one of the ways we hold on to hope.

There are times when I come to worship to affirm the faith that I hold, but there are other times when I come to worship so that the faith the church affirms can hold me. There are times when I come to sing my song of hope, but there are other times when I need the church to sing that song for me. There are times when I am present with my small group in order to encourage someone else, and there are times when I need to be present so they can encourage me.

Our Presence in Community

The Old Testament book of Ecclesiastes provides a visual image of what it means for us to be present in Christian community with a small group of fellow disciples: "Two are better than one. . . . For if they fall, one will lift up the other. . . . A threefold cord is not quickly broken" (Ecclesiastes 4:9-12).

All praise to our redeeming Lord,
who joins us by his grace,
and bids us, each to each restored,
together seek his face.

He bids us build each other up;
and, gathered into one,
to our high calling's glorious hope
we hand in hand go on.

And if our fellowship below
in Jesus be so sweet,
what height of rapture shall we know
when round his throne we meet!
—Charles Wesley[7]

The first Methodists both believed and practiced that principle. When Benjamin Ingham came for his first visit with John Wesley, he was already involved with a small group of Oxford students who were searching for a holy life. He came to Wesley for practical guidance on how they could more effectively "provoke one another to love and good deeds" (Hebrews 10:24).

John and Charles Wesley were already engaged in similar groups that tracked their origin to the religious societies that had begun to emerge in England in the 1670s. The purpose of these groups was to counteract the widespread spiritual apathy and casual immorality of the time by promoting holiness of heart and life.[6]

The small groups at Oxford were the first examples of the kinds of small groups that Wesley would later organize into a network of "class meetings," "bands," and "societies." These groups would become the organizational genius of the Methodist movement. When the movement had grown to the point that John Wesley was preaching to thousands of people at a time, he observed that those who were active participants in the smaller groups continued to grow in their faith, while those who were not engaged in such a group quickly fell away.[8]

That principle is just as true today as it was in eighteenth-century England. The evidence is clear that if an individual's only contact with the congregation is worship, there is a good chance that he or she either will fall away or will miss out on the concern and care of the church community. Growth to maturity as a disciple of Jesus Christ happens best when each individual disciple is connected to others in the community of a small group.

Small-group community can happen in a variety of ways. *A Disciple's Path Daily Workbook* outlines one pattern for small-group community based on the form of Wesley Groups. Other small-group formats include Disciple Bible Study, Covenant Discipleship Groups, and traditional Sunday school classes—in addition to a myriad of options your church might offer. One of the goals of our congregation is to turn "committees" into "communities" by engaging committee members in sharing their own spiritual journeys, being deeply united in prayer, and becoming a network of concern and care for one another.

Larry's story continues through his presence in the men's group where he experiences the trust, accountability, and intimacy of a small group. An equally important element of his growth has been his consistent presence in worship, where he is drawn beyond himself and beyond the intimate circle of his small group into God's presence with the gathered congregation. Worship turns our attention away from ourselves and toward God.

Our Presence in Worship

From the earliest days of the Methodist movement at Oxford, John and Charles Wesley insisted that the Methodist people be faithful in worship in the Church of England. Benjamin Ingham's diary confirms his daily attendance at morning and evening prayer at Oxford. He was present for the services on every saint's day or festival in the Anglican liturgical calendar and was persistent in following Wesley's guidance to receive the sacrament as often as possible. On Sundays he was present with other Oxford Methodists for the Eucharist at Christ Church or at the Oxford Castle prison.[9] What other Oxford students considered as obsessive attendance at worship was one of the practices that brought scorn and mockery on these first Methodists.

Years later, as the movement spread across England, Wesley continued to encourage the Methodists to receive the sacraments in the Anglican Church until they were forced out of many congregations. When he wrote "The Nature, Design, and General Rules of the United Societies," Wesley's third rule was "attend upon the ordinances of God."[10]

From the very beginning, being present in corporate worship and sharing in the sacrament of Holy Communion have held a central place in the Wesleyan understanding of discipleship.

In his book *Treasures of the Transformed Life*, John Ed Mathison tells the story of a Sunday morning when an ice storm shut down Montgomery, Alabama.[11] Church leaders wondered whether anyone would be present for worship at Frazer Memorial United Methodist Church. Mathison was amazed when he saw one of the older women of the congregation making her way across the ice to the church. He told her he was surprised that she decided to come to worship on that icy morning. Quick to teach him a lesson, she told him that if she had waited until Sunday morning to decide whether she would be in worship, she might not have come. But she made that decision the previous fall when she made a commitment to be in worship forty-eight Sundays that year. She knew the four Sundays she planned to be out of town, and this wasn't one of them. She had made a commitment to be in worship, and she intended to keep it. While acknowledging his concern for her safety, Mathison shared the story as an example of a personal commitment to corporate worship.

The Work of Worship

When Woody Allen said that "80 percent of success is showing up,"[12] he wasn't talking about worship. There's more to being present in worship than simply showing up on Sunday morning. Worship is not a performance we watch but an experience we share. Being fully present means entering into the liturgy, which comes from the medieval Latin phrase meaning "the work of the people."[13] Our active participation in worship becomes the practice by which we break free from self-centered existence and discover a Christ-centered life. The Apostle Paul's letter to the Ephesians gives us a glimpse into that experience.

Paul wrote, "Do not get drunk with wine" (Ephesians 5:18). In the teetotaling, abstinence-pledge-signing church in which I grew up, we knew exactly what Paul meant. Given the massive abuse of alcohol in our culture today, it is still a word we need to hear. But the apostle's concern in writing to the Ephesians was not so much the abuse of alcohol as the abuse of worship.

The Ephesian Christians lived in a Greek culture that was saturated with all sorts of religious options. One of these was the worship of Dionysus, the god of wine. Worship of Dionysius involved consuming massive amounts of wine to the point of total intoxication, often resulting in drunken orgies. Paul was drawing a contrast between the pagan worship of Dionysius and Christian worship when he wrote, "Do not get drunk with wine, for that is debauchery, *but* be filled with the Holy Spirit" (Ephesians 5:18, emphasis added).

In contrast to the raucous debauchery and disorder of the worship of Dionysius, Paul described the beauty, harmony, and order of worship in the early church: "As you sing psalms and hymns and spiritual songs among yourselves, singing and making melody to the Lord in your hearts, giving thanks to God the Father at all times and for everything in the name of our Lord Jesus Christ" (Ephesians 5:19-20).

Just as Paul peeks in on the worship of the church in Ephesus, let's look in on worship in The United Methodist Church to discover what it might mean for our worship to be filled, soaked, intoxicated with the spirit of God.

A hopeful sign of renewal within The United Methodist Church is the growth of an almost staggering array of worship forms and experiences in local churches that are intentionally redesigning their worship services in order to more effectively reach people in their communities who have not yet experienced the love of God in Christ. For some congregations and pastors, it is not unlike John Wesley saying that he "submitted to be more vile"[14] by following George Whitefield to preach in the fields and coal mines of England, or Charles Wesley setting his hymns to familiar tunes in order to share the good news with the common people. But whatever the style of music, worship in the Methodist tradition draws on four essential elements outlined in *The United Methodist Book of Worship* and *The United Methodist Hymnal*.

1. The Gathering of the Church

When we worship, we come from all the ordinary places and patterns of our lives to enter into an extraordinary place and time when our attention is drawn out of the narrow confines of our self-interest and into the presence of God.

The Apostle Paul heard the call to worship in the words of the Old Testament prophet Isaiah:

> Sleeper, awake!
> Rise from the dead,
> and Christ will shine on you. (Ephesians 5:14)

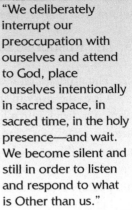

We are so easily intoxicated with the values, attitudes, and priorities of the world that we might as well be asleep to the presence of God. Worship begins by awakening us from the intoxicating stupor of the culture around us. We are called to wake up to what God has done and is doing in Jesus Christ.

> "We deliberately interrupt our preoccupation with ourselves and attend to God, place ourselves intentionally in sacred space, in sacred time, in the holy presence—and wait. We become silent and still in order to listen and respond to what is Other than us."
> —Eugene Peterson[15]

The awakening begins before we enter the building. At Hyde Park we talk about hospitality "from the street to the seat" as a means by which the Holy Spirit begins to work in people's lives. We are awakened by the warmth of the welcome, the physical setting in which we worship, the music we hear, and the first words that are spoken to call the congregation into the presence of God.

And we do it together. It matters that we are in worship with others. We can have individualized religious experiences watching the sun rise over the mountains or watching the sun set into the ocean. But we cannot experience the fullness of Christian worship by ourselves. We do it together with brothers and sisters in Christ whom we do not choose and who are drawn together in the name of Christ.

2. The Proclamation of the Word

Once we have gathered and have awakened to the presence of God, we are ready to hear the proclamation of the word. We are people of the book, people who have been given a story to tell. We didn't make this up on our own. It's a story that was given to us.

While I was working on this book, my family went to Pennsylvania for a family reunion. My children and grandchildren met relatives they had never seen before. As it happens in every family reunion, we told old family stories—the stories that remind us of who we are. And as we heard the stories, they became our own; we found our place in them, and we passed them on. That's part of what happens when we read Scripture and proclaim the word in worship.

The church I serve was founded in 1899. When the first group of Methodists gathered on our corner, they sang the old hymn that says, "I love to tell the story of . . . Jesus and his love."[16] That's what we do. We tell the story of what God has done and is doing in Christ. We tell the story that shapes and forms us as disciples of Christ. We proclaim the good news that invites others to experience God's love in Christ.

Sometimes we tell the story through preaching. Sometimes we tell it through music, dance, or drama. Sometimes we tell it through creative media that engage the senses. Whatever forms we use, we tell the story in order to find our place within it so that the story becomes our own.

3. The Response to the Word

The proclamation of the word calls for our response.

I love the story of the guy who kept going to sleep in church. The preacher wanted to teach him a lesson, so he said very softly, "Everyone who wants to go to heaven, raise your hand." The whole congregation quietly raised their hands, except for this guy who was sound asleep in the back of the church. Then the preacher said, "Everyone who wants to go to hell, *stand up!*" The slumbering saint jumped up, looked around, and said, "Preacher, I'm not sure what we are voting on, but it looks like we're the only two in favor of it."

There are better ways to respond. We respond in thanksgiving to God for all that God has done and in commitment to Jesus Christ. And that brings us to the offering.

The primary purpose of the offering in Christian worship is not to raise money for the church. The giving of our gifts is the symbol of the giving of ourselves. It is the act of worship in which we say thanks to God for all that God has done in Christ and in which we offer ourselves—our prayers, our presence, our gifts, our service, and our witness—in commitment to Jesus Christ.

I grew up on the camp meeting branch of the American Methodist tradition in which the most typical form of response was the altar call. The sermon always ended with a clear call to commitment and the invitation to come to the Communion rail where someone would be prepared to pray with us about the step we were taking in our faith. It's still a meaningful form of response for people who are ready to make new commitments to Christ or who need to experience prayers for healing, comfort, wisdom, or strength.

Sometimes the response takes a very specific form related to the overall theme of the text and the occasion. On the tenth anniversary of the 9/11 attacks, everyone who came to worship received a small chunk of concrete. I began the sermon by showing the congregation a chunk of the World Trade Center that was given to me by a person who helped in the recovery. During the offering and the closing hymn, we invited people to bring the piece of concrete in their hands and lay it on the altar as a way of releasing some of their pain, bitterness, revenge, or fear to God.

We also respond in thanksgiving and commitment as we gather at the table and receive the bread and cup, the body and blood of our Lord Jesus Christ. Eucharist means "thanksgiving." It's the central act of the church in which we once again hear the story of what God has done in Christ and offer ourselves in thanks and praise.[17]

I heard about a father who took his young son to worship in a church where they served Communion by passing the cups in the pews. His son took the little cup in his hand, lifted it up to his father, and said, "Cheers!"

His response was not all that far removed from that moment at the Last Supper when Jesus said, "Be of good cheer; I have overcome the world" (John 16:33 KJV). Christian worship is a countercultural gathering in which we declare that the risen Christ has overcome every power that would separate us, every force that would divide us, and every evil that would destroy us. In worship we declare that Jesus Christ is Lord over all.

4. The Sending Forth

As worship concludes, we are sent forth into the world in the confidence of the risen Christ. The church gathered for worship becomes the church scattered for witness and service. Having heard the story of God's love in Christ, we are sent out to make that love real to others. We come in to prepare to be sent out. Worship is like the locker room where players prepare to be sent onto the field.

In addition to Paul's words to the Ephesians, there is another place in Scripture where disciples were accused of being drunk. On the day of Pentecost, when the frightened and fearful followers of Jesus were filled with the Holy Spirit and began telling the story of Jesus so that people from all around the world could hear and understand it, Luke records that everyone was "amazed and perplexed, saying to one another, 'What does this mean?' But others sneered and said, 'They are filled with new wine'" (Acts 2:12-13).

But Peter responded, "These are not drunk, as you suppose, for it is only nine o'clock in the morning" (Acts 2:15). Peter went on to explain that this was the fulfillment of the words of the prophet Joel that one day God would pour out God's spirit so that everyone could be filled, saturated, intoxicated with the spirit of God.

In New Testament times, the worship of Dionysus—like far too much of what passes for worship in our culture today—was all about "me." It was about being intoxicated with your own spiritual experience. But Christian worship is not about you or me. It's about our lives being transformed, filled with the spirit of Jesus Christ so that we become the agents of his love, joy, and peace in this world. We are sent into the world as men and women who are intoxicated with the spirit of God and empowered by the risen Christ to become the people through whom God's kingdom comes and God's will gets done on earth as it is in heaven.

Our presence in Christian community and in corporate worship really matters. It matters to us because it is one of the essential practices by which we are formed into the likeness of Christ. It matters to others because our presence may be the gift that God uses to strengthen, encourage, challenge, and bless our brothers and sisters in Christ. It matters to the world because it prepares us to become the agents of God's persistent love as we participate in God's transformation of the world!

CHAPTER 4

Money Matters
Financial Generosity

An article in *The Harvard Business Review* caught my attention. Writing to business leaders in the summer when the United States debt crisis converged with the highly hyped release of the final Harry Potter movie, Umair Haque acknowledged that he was captivated by the possibility of a magical world in which a few memorized incantations could miraculously resolve our economic crisis.

Unfortunately, Haque said, "In our messy muggle world, there are no magic formulas." He wrote:

> Great achievement, deep fulfillment, lasting relationships, or any other aspects of an unquenchably, relentlessly well lived life aren't formulaically executable or neatly quantifiable. First and foremost, they're searingly, and deeply personally, meaningful. The inconvenient truth is: you'll probably have to not just blaze your own trail—you'll also probably have to plot your own map for [your] own journey.[1]

If we were to apply Haque's words to the task of following the discipleship pathway, he would be partially correct. A well-lived life in which we love God with our whole hearts, minds, souls, and strength and love others the way we have been loved by God is not the result of a magical incantation. Nor is it "formulaically executable or neatly quantifiable."

On the other hand, we are not left to "blaze [our] own trail" or draw our own map for the journey. Our destination was revealed in the life, death, and resurrection of Jesus, "the pioneer and perfecter of our faith" (Hebrews 12:2). The trail has been blazed by generations of saints and sinners who have traveled this road before us.

And we do not make the journey alone. We travel in the company of other faithful disciples who, in the words of our baptismal covenant, "surround [us] with a community of love and forgiveness" so that we may "grow in [our] trust of God, and be found faithful in [our] service to others." We live with sisters and brothers who have vowed to pray for one another so that we may become "true disciples who walk in the way that leads to life."[2]

John Wesley guided the early Methodists along a path that combined absolute trust in the transforming work of the spirit of God with practical guidance on the methods that enable us to become disciples who are equipped to participate in God's transformation of the world.

I'm sure Mr. Haque did not have discipleship or Methodists in mind, but he was within arm's reach of Wesley's convictions when he said that this is the place to begin: "Put *what, why,* and *who* you love ahead of what, why, and who you *don't,* and your roadmap will begin to write itself."[3] He warned that in our frantic pursuit of "more, bigger, faster, cheaper, nastier," the tragic result is that we end up putting "what, why, and who we love" at the end of the list. He concluded that the roadmap we need to follow is one that leads us "somewhere that matters—not just somewhere that glitters."[4]

The Wesleyan way of discipleship is focused on the love of God at work in the core of who we are and the things we love. It puts what we love, who we are, and why we are here at the center of what we believe and the way we act. Wesley's methodical approach to the Christian life gives us a practical roadmap that leads in the direction of a life in which everything we say and do is organized around loving God and loving others. And that includes what we do with our money.

When Methodists Started Making Money

The unexpected result of the methodical way of life that Wesley modeled and taught was that by living cleaner, better educated, and more disciplined lives, the Methodists started making money. They began to accumulate wealth, wear fine clothing, and build more attractive preaching houses. In 1760, Wesley responded with his sermon "The Use of Money," followed by his sermons "On the Danger of Riches" and "On the Danger of Increasing Riches."[5]

When Wesley wrote these sermons, he was not fund-raising for the Methodist movement. He accomplished that purpose through his network of societies and class meetings. The motivation for Wesley's sermons was his desire to lead the Methodist people into more Christ-centered lives. He was not going after their money; he was going for their hearts and souls. The sermons are rooted in the conviction that we cannot be faithful disciples of Jesus Christ unless we learn to manage the "excellent gift" of money, as Wesley called it, wisely and "to the greatest advantage."[7]

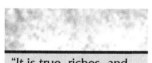

"It is true, riches, and the increase of them, are the gift of God. Yet great care is to be taken, that what is intended for a blessing, do not turn into a curse."

—John Wesley[6]

To accomplish his purpose, Wesley laid out three simple rules in his sermon "The Use of Money": gain all you can; save all you can; and give all you can.[8] Let's look at each rule briefly. (For a deeper study, see my book *Simple Rules for Money* [Nashville: Abingdon Press, 2010].)

"Gain All You Can"

Wesley began his sermon with a good word about money. He called it "an excellent gift of God" and challenged his followers "to employ it to the greatest advantage."[9] He said that "Gain all you can" is the first rule of Christian wisdom related to money, and he told us how to do it:

> Use all possible diligence in your calling. Lose no time. . . . Never leave anything till to-morrow, which you can do to-day. And do it as well as possible. . . . Put your whole strength to the work. . . . Let nothing be done by halves, or in a slight and careless manner. . . . Do everything you have to do better to-day than you did yesterday. . . . Make the best of all that is in your hands.[10]

Whew! Wesley's work ethic can wear out even a recovering workaholic like me! It's no wonder that the early Methodists became productive and prosperous. Lifted out of a biblical context, Wesley's words could encourage a lifestyle driven by what Haque called "more, bigger, faster, cheaper." Gain all we can, in every way we can, as quickly as we can, with as little responsibility and as few constraints as we can is the mantra of our consumer culture. That's not what Wesley had in mind. He said that we should gain all we can "without paying more for it than it is worth.[11]

To be sure that the Methodists didn't pay too high a price for their wealth, he put several boundaries around their efforts that are still applicable for us today:

- **Gain all you can without hurting your health.** That's a good word in a culture where too many of us are working ourselves to death for money.

- **Gain all you can without hurting your mind.** Wesley warned against any business that would involve cheating, lying, or engaging in behavior that is not consistent with a good conscience. Those are wise words for many of us who are constantly tempted to do things that we know are inconsistent with the values of a Christian life.

- **Gain all you can without hurting your neighbor.** Loving others as we love ourselves requires that we consider the way our economic practices will impact others. Wesley was emphatic that "none can gain by swallowing up his neighbour's substance, without gaining the damnation of hell!"[12] It's the opposite principle of Daddy Warbucks, who told Annie that you don't have to be nice to the people you pass on the way up if you don't intend to come back down.

With those cautions in place, Wesley called us to gain all we can by doing everything better each day and making the best of what we have in our hands.

"Save All You Can"

Wesley's second rule was "Save all you can." When Wesley called the early Methodists to save all that they could, he wasn't talking about hoarding money in a savings account or stuffing it in a mattress. He was describing a lifestyle that we might call "frugal." Coming from the Latin root meaning "useful, temperate," *frugal* is defined as "living without waste."[13]

Wesley told his followers not to waste their money on superfluous, overly expensive, or needless purchases, which led the early Methodists to a plain, practical, simple lifestyle. He warned them about what we would call "compulsive" shopping—an addiction that pervades our culture today—when he said, "The more they are indulged, they increase the more."[15]

The purpose of Wesley's rule to save all we can is not to amass a huge savings account but to discover the contentment that Paul described to the Philippians when he said,

> I have learned to be content with whatever I have. I know what it is to have little, and I know what it is to have plenty. In any and all circumstances I have learned the secret of being well-fed and of going hungry, of having plenty and of being in need. I can do all things through him who strengthens me. (Philippians 4:11-13)

"Give All You Can"

Wesley's rules on the use of money are progressive. Gaining all we can and saving all we can are steps in the direction of a generous life in which we give all we can.

Wesley's challenge to give all we can goes far deeper than just writing a check to charity. The purpose of the discipline of generosity is for our lives to be shaped into the likeness of the extravagant generosity of God. To use Umair Haque's words, it's about *what, why,* and *who* we love. It's following a roadmap that leads us to something that really matters, "not just something that glitters."[16]

The Tragic Trap of Possessions

The practical importance of Wesley's rules on money and possessions came home to me when I discovered the story of Homer and Langley Collyer. They were teenagers when their family moved into the three-story brownstone on Fifth Avenue in New York City in 1909, and that's where they died in 1947.

When an anonymous caller reported that there was a dead body in the house, police were unable to get in because of the mountains of junk piled behind the doors. They broke in through a second-story window and found the entire house packed with stuff from wall to wall, floor to ceiling. Digging through tons of material on the ground floor alone, they found Homer's body. Almost three weeks later they discovered Langley's body, crushed under one of the booby traps he had set to protect their possessions.

Authorities eventually removed 130 tons of junk from the house, including decades of old newspapers, broken-down furniture, the chassis of a Model T, fourteen pianos, and more than twenty-five thousand books.[17]

The Collyer brothers were obviously suffering from severe mental illness, but their tragic story is not unlike some of the stories that Jesus told. Jesus never hesitated to use bold contrasts, visual hyperbole, and shocking exaggeration to demonstrate the difference between life under the reign and rule of God's love and life under the values and assumptions of the culture around us. He used a spiritual force field analysis in which he forces us to choose between mutually exclusive alternatives, particularly in speaking about wealth and possessions. His words in the sixth chapter of Matthew could be a commentary on the tragedy of the Collyer brothers: "Do not store up for yourselves treasures on earth, where moth and rust consume and where thieves break in and steal; but store up for yourselves treasures in heaven, where neither moth nor rust consumes and where thieves do not break in and steal" (Matthew 6:19-20).

Observe that Jesus does not draw the contrast between "storing up" on the one hand and "not storing up" on the other. Like Wesley saying that we should gain all we can, Jesus assumes that we share an innate desire to acquire, possess, and hold things to which we give value.

The question is *where* we will store our things. Will we invest our resources in things that are temporary and transitory—things that fade away? Or will we invest in things that last forever? Jesus makes his point in verse 21: "For where your treasure is, there your heart will be also."

I wish Jesus had said that where one's heart is determines where one's treasure will be. But he said that if we really want to know where our hearts are—in other words, what we most deeply value and love—all we need to do is follow the money.

In verses 22-23, Jesus forces us to think about the way we look at the world, the perspective through which we view our lives: "The eye is the lamp of the body. So, if your eye is healthy, your whole body will be full of light; but if your eye is unhealthy, your whole body will be full of darkness. If then the light in you is darkness, how great is the darkness!"

In this little lesson on optometry, Jesus was drawing on an Old Testament proverb that would have been familiar to his first hearers. The writer of Proverbs uses the eye to describe the lens through which we see and experience the world.

It's the basic orientation of our existence, the fundamental perspective by which we determine reality.

The book of Proverbs says that there are two kinds of eyes:

> He that hath a *bountiful eye* shall be blessed; for he giveth of his bread to the poor. (Proverbs 22:9 KJV, emphasis added)

> He that hasteth to be rich hath an *evil eye*, and considereth not that poverty shall come upon him. (Proverbs 28:22 KJV, emphasis added)

The "bountiful eye" looks out on the world from a perspective of generosity. It sees life through the lens of giving and sharing life with others. In contrast, the "evil eye" is the greedy eye, the eye that is turned in on itself and measures all of reality from the perspective of its self-interest.

Jesus evidently was using this proverb to say that we get to choose. We can look at life through a "bountiful" eye with a spirit of generosity toward others, or we can look at life through the narrow lens of our self-interest. Jesus said that if your eye is healthy—if you have the "bountiful" eye—your whole body will be full of light, but if you have the "evil" eye, your whole life will be filled with darkness. We can choose the "eye" through which we see reality.

Jesus' strongest word about money draws on the metaphor of slavery: "No one can serve two masters; for a slave will either hate the one and love the other, or be devoted to the one and despise the other. You cannot serve God and wealth" (Matthew 6:24).

The New Revised Standard Version and other newer translations use the words *wealth* and *money*. The King James Version uses the word *mammon*, which accomplishes exactly what Jesus wanted: it personifies money, portraying mammon as a competing idol, a force that competes with God for the ultimate loyalty of our lives.

Jesus is forcing us to choose which god we will serve—which god will have the ultimate loyalty of our lives. The choice is always between God, whose generosity is so great that God pours out sun and rain on both the just and the unjust, and mammon, the self-destructive acquisitive passion that measures everything by its self-interest.

Jesus forces the decision on us: Who will be the Master of our lives? Whom will we serve? Will we use our possessions to serve God's purpose, or will we use our lives to serve our possessions? Will we surrender the control of our lives to our possessions, or will we surrender our possessions to the control of the God of infinite generosity?

We can summarize Jesus' force field analysis in these questions:

- Where is your heart?
- How are your eyes? Through which lens do you see?
- Whom do you serve?

In one of the most beautiful passages in Matthew's Gospel, Jesus describes the alternative of life that is centered in loving God and loving others:

> I tell you, do not worry about your life, what you will eat or what you will drink, or about your body, what you will wear. Is not life more than food, and the body more than clothing? Look at the birds of the air; they neither sow nor reap nor gather into barns, and yet your heavenly Father feeds them. Are you not of more value than they? And can any of you by worrying add a single hour to your span of life? And why do you worry about clothing? Consider the lilies of the field, how they grow; they neither toil nor spin, yet I tell you, even Solomon in all his glory was not clothed like one of these. But if God so clothes the grass of the field, which is alive today and tomorrow is thrown into the oven, will he not much more clothe you—you of little faith? Therefore do not worry, saying, "What will we eat?" or "What will we drink?" or "What will we wear?" For it is the Gentiles who strive for all these things; and indeed your heavenly Father knows that you need all these things. But strive first for the kingdom of God and his righteousness, and all these things will be given to you as well. (Matthew 6:25-33)

If only Homer and Langley Collyer had believed that. What a difference it might have made in their lives. What difference will it make in yours?

Practicing Generosity

In light of Wesley's rules and Jesus' teaching, here are my "plain rules" about the spiritual discipline of financial generosity:

- **Generosity begins with God.** Generosity begins not with what I give to God, but with what God has given to me. The Bible says that extravagant, self-giving generosity is the tangible expression of the love that is in the very heart of God. We are generous to others because God has been so extravagantly generous to us.

- **Generosity is essential.** Generosity is not optional for followers of Jesus Christ. It is the spiritual discipline that shapes our lives around the extravagant generosity of God. Our use of money undergoes a fundamental transformation when we stop asking how much of our wealth we will give to God and start asking how much of God's wealth we will keep for ourselves. Generosity is the only antidote to greed, which is one of the seven deadly sins. Greed is sinful because it is an inherent contradiction of the essential character of God. It is deadly because it results in spiritual arteriosclerosis that blocks the flow of God's life into our lives and into the world.

- **Generosity is intentional.** It doesn't just happen. We don't become generous unless we plan for it. If I decide to be generous at the end of my spending, there won't be anything left to spend. That's where tithing comes in. The biblical practice of giving the first 10 percent of what we earn for God's work in the world is a spiritual discipline that enables us to build consistent generosity into our financial lifestyle and becomes the base line or beginning point for a generous life.

- **Generosity grows with practice.** It is a learned behavior that runs against the grain of the predominant mood of our culture. It is a spiritual discipline that, if practiced over time, will enable us to break free from a self-centered life and grow into a Christ-centered one.

- **Generosity is joyful.** I've observed that, generally speaking, generous people are joyful and stingy people are grouches. When we give all we can, we experience the joy of knowing that through our generosity, we share in the way God is blessing our lives and the lives of others. My giving enables me to get in on God's transformation of this world into something like the kingdom of God.

- **Generosity results in blessing.** I can't promise that if you tithe, you will get rich. I can promise that if you develop the spiritual practice of generosity, you will be blessed, and your life will become a blessing to others. Ultimately a generous heart is its own reward.

The world of the generous gets larger and larger;
    the world of the stingy gets smaller and smaller.
The one who blesses others is abundantly blessed;
    those who help others are helped.
    —Proverbs 11:24-25
    THE MESSAGE

My pastoral observation and personal experience confirm that although Mr. Haque was not thinking of discipleship when he wrote his article in *The Harvard Business Review*, he got it right when he said that the key to "an unquenchably, relentlessly well lived life" is found only in putting what we love ahead of everything else. When we get our wealth and possessions in line with loving God and loving others, we are on the road that leads toward "somewhere that matters—not just somewhere that glitters."[18]

CHAPTER 5

The Way of Service
Spiritual Gifts and Gifts-based Service

On May 16, 2006, the auctioneer at Christie's in London held up an old violin and opened the bidding. There were audible gasps when bids passed $1 million and then $2 million. When the bidding ended at $3.5 million, the typically sedate auction house broke into applause. It was the highest price that ever had been paid for a musical instrument.[1]

Here's why. The violin had been hand-crafted in 1707 by Antonio Stradivari, the greatest maker of stringed instruments in history. No other instrument produces the quality of sound that comes from a Stradivarius, though no one has fully explained why.

Mary Anne Evans, the nineteenth-century British novelist and poet who used the pen name George Eliot to make sure that her works were taken seriously, wrote a poem in which she described Stradivarius as a simple man who patiently worked at his bench for forty years.

In the poem, a young, undisciplined painter named Naldo mocks Antonio's hard work, telling him that he could have wealth and fame with a lot less labor. Antonio replies that any musician who holds one of his violins will be grateful that Stradivari lived, made violins, and made them the best that he could. He says that God gives the musicians their skill, but he gives them instruments to play: "God choosing me to help Him."[2]

When Naldo is shocked by the idea that God needs Antonio's help, Antonio replies,

> *Not God Himself can make man's best*
> *Without best men to help Him. . . .*
> *. . . He could not make*
> *Antonio Stradivari's violins*
> *Without Antonio.*[3]

The poet captured this shocking affirmation of Scripture: the infinite, almighty God chooses to accomplish the transformation of the world by working in and through the lives of ordinary people who become the agents of God's love.

Participants in God's Transformation of the World

I am confident that the almighty God is fully capable of saving, redeeming, and setting right everything that has gone wrong in this world by God's own power. I'm sure that God's kingdom could come and God's will could be done on earth solely by God's own power. But the God revealed in the Bible is the God who chooses to bring that kingdom to reality through the gifts and energies of ordinary folks such as us.

"Each gift is an invitation and provides the means to participate in the work of Jesus. . . . We are being invited into a working relationship in the operations of the Trinity."
—Eugene Peterson[4]

In the book of Genesis, God made a covenant with Abraham and Sarah, through whom God promised that all the nations of the earth would be blessed. God stuck with that covenant through thick and thin, ultimately entering into our humanity in Jesus Christ. After Jesus' death and resurrection, God breathed life into the church, the body of Christ, to become the covenant community through which God's kingdom will come and God's will, will be done on earth as it is in heaven. The church is

- more than another helping agency in the community.
- more than a body of like-minded people doing good things in this world by the combination of their human interests and talents.
- intended by God to be nothing less than the tangible expression of God's rule and reign in this world.
- a divinely formed community of disciples, called into being by the spirit of God and energized by that same Spirit to accomplish God's work through God's own power.

"The true vocation of every believer . . . is a summons to enter a particular, revolutionary path of self-sacrificing love for the world. To be the church . . . is to accept Jesus' invitation to participate in a new age of peace with justice founded upon the reckless abandonment of power and self."
—Paul Wesley Chilcote[5]

The good news is that God has not left us to do God's work alone. Jesus promised that he would send the Holy Spirit who not only would be *with us*, but also would be *in us*, enabling us to become that which we can never become on our own (see John 14:15-17).

Just as God could not make Antonio Stradivari's violins without Antonio, so God cannot make this world what God wants it to become without God's people. At the same time, we cannot become the servant people God intends the church to be without the presence, power, and direction of the Holy Spirit.

If we want to experience the life that God intends for us, there comes a point where we shift from being merely recipients of grace to being channels of grace to others. If we want to continue growing into a life that is centered on loving God and loving others, there comes a time when we no longer hold God's love for ourselves but find ways to share it with others. If we want to live a life worthy of our high calling, there comes a point where we stop being spectators and become participants in God's transformation of the world.

To Each a Gift

It's amazing enough to believe that God chooses to accomplish the transformation of the world through the lives of ordinary men and women who become disciples of Jesus Christ. Equally amazing is the way God does it. The Holy Spirit equips every baptized follower of Christ to become the agent of God's love in the world by giving each of us unique spiritual gifts that become the means by which God's kingdom comes and God's will is done in and through our lives. In his letter to the Ephesians, the Apostle Paul lays the biblical foundation for the practice of gifts-based service (Ephesians 4:1-16). A careful study of the passage uncovers five basic principles regarding the use of these gifts.

1. Every follower of Christ is united with every other follower of Christ in the one mission of the church.

The apostle begins with a bold affirmation of the unity of the church by calling us to bear with one another in love by making every effort "to maintain the unity of the Spirit in the bond of peace" (Ephesians 4:3). Paul declares this common mission of the body of Christ by lifting a piece of liturgy out of the worship life of the early church. It may have been an affirmation of faith or a part of the baptismal liturgy: "There is one body and one Spirit, just as you were called to the one hope of your calling, one Lord, one faith, one baptism, one God and Father of all, who is above all and through all and in all" (Ephesians 4:4-6).

It would be impossible to miss his use of the word one. It appears seven times in that single sentence, and it is reinforced by his repetition of the word all in the final phrase.

Paul wants there to be no doubt that there are no solo performers in the orchestra of God's grace, no starring actors in the drama of God's love. We are bound together in the oneness of the body of Christ.

2. Every follower of Jesus Christ has been given a gift.

Having clearly established the oneness of the church, the apostle immediately declares that "each of us was given grace according to the measure of Christ's gift" (Ephesians 4:7). He balances the oneness of the body with the uniqueness of our individual gifts. He reaffirms this principle when he tells the Corinthians,

"There are varieties of gifts, but the same Spirit; and there are varieties of services, but the same Lord; and there are varieties of activities, but it is the same God who activates all of them in everyone" (1 Corinthians 12:4-6).

As United Methodists, we live into this combination of the oneness of the Body and the uniqueness of each disciple's gifts in what the *Discipline* calls "The Ministry of All Christians." We declare that we believe that every Christian disciple is called to the ministry of servanthood through his or her baptism. We are one in Christ through the gift of grace that is symbolized in the water of baptism. The *Discipline* goes on to affirm that "God's gifts are richly diverse for a variety of services; yet all have dignity and worth."[6]

Paul gives us a taste of the rich diversity of gifts when he says that some disciples are gifted to be apostles, some evangelists, some pastors and teachers. In the letter to Corinth, he expands the options to include gifts of wisdom, knowledge, faith, healing, miracles, prophecy, discernment, tongues, and interpretation of tongues (1 Corinthians 12:8-11). Other lists of gifts are included in *A Disciple's Path Daily Workbook* along with instructions for using an online assessment tool that can help each disciple find his or her unique set of gifts.

3. Every gift makes a difference.

Paul tells us that no gift is insignificant. Every gift is absolutely essential in God's transformation of the world.

The *Discipline* affirms that the gifts of God in the lives of disciples are complementary. No one gift is better than or more important than another. We are called by God and sent into the world as fellow servants who need one another's gifts for our gifts to be complete.[7] Every gift makes a difference in God's work of transformation in the world.

I learned the lesson that every gift is important from my college drama professor. Before announcing who had received parts in the new production, she would remind us that there are no small parts, only small actors. That's how it is in the body of Christ. There are no small parts or insignificant gifts. Every gift matters in the body of Christ.

4. Every gift is given for the common good.

Paul tells the Corinthians that every unique gift is "the manifestation of the Spirit for the common good" (1 Corinthians 12:7). No gift is given to draw attention to itself, but every gift is given "for building up the body of Christ" so that every individual disciple will grow to maturity in the likeness of Jesus Christ (Ephesians 4:11-15).

Paul's classic illustration of this principle is his comparison of the body of Christ to the human body (1 Corinthians 12:12-27). I sense him writing with bold satire, making a mockery of the very idea that a foot would say, "Because I am not a hand, I do not belong to the body" (verse 15). He laughs at the lunacy of an ear saying, "Because I am not an eye, I do not belong to the body" (verse 16). What kind of sense would that be? He asks the outrageous question, "If all were a single member, where would the body be?" (verse 19).

Then, while he has his reader laughing at the absurdity of such an arrogant possibility, he brings his point home: "If one member suffers, all suffer together with it; if one member is honored, all rejoice together with it" (verse 26). And he nails his argument with this final conclusion: "Now you are the body of Christ and individually members of it" (verse 27). Case closed. Argument over. We are called to exercise our gifts fully and freely, knowing that no one gift is complete by itself. All of us are in this business together!

5. Every follower of Christ becomes a coworker with God in God's transformation of this world when we discover and use our gifts.

By the use of our gifts, we become a part in God's answer to the prayer that God's kingdom will come and God's will, will be done on earth as it is in heaven.

The *Discipline* concludes with disturbing clarity about the importance of using our gifts in service. It declares that the people of God—ordinary people like every one of us—must either convince the world of the reality of the gospel or leave the world unconvinced. That's a tall order! As if that were not challenging enough, it tells us that we can neither evade this responsibility nor delegate it to someone else. It leaves us with this unsettling alternative: "The church is either faithful as a witnessing and serving community, or it loses its vitality and its impact on an unbelieving world."[8]

A *Disciple's Path Daily Workbook* provides practical steps by which we can discover the gifts the Holy Spirit has placed in our lives and begin to discern the specific ways in which those gifts can be used in service to others. Dr. Donald English, who for many years was the spiritual leader of Methodism in Great Britain, used to say that the world doesn't need any more salespersons for the gospel; all the world needs is more free samples. So, let me share with you three examples of the way ordinary disciples have discovered their gifts and become part of God's transformation of the world.

Example #1: Prepared by Prayer

I called one of our senior adults on behalf of the Committee on Lay Leadership to talk with her about becoming the new lay leader of our congregation. Before I could tell her why I called, she said, "I've been praying for God to lead me, and I'm ready to say yes to just about anything." Her comment revealed the way her practice of the spiritual discipline of prayer and reflection on Scripture had prepared her to hear and respond to God's call when it came. We talked about why the committee believed that this role might match her gifts. She confirmed that it did, and she gave excellent leadership to our congregation.

Any movement in the direction of gifts-based service is rooted in a consistent life of prayer.

Example #2: Using the Gift You're Given

An attorney and lifelong Methodist had been actively involved in many ways in the congregation. When we began focusing attention on discovering spiritual gifts, he used the assessment instrument, which revealed his primary gift to be administration. He said he really had hoped for a more exciting gift, so he took the assessment again. He used another instrument for a third time. The assessments came out with the same result each time: administration.

He was frustrated and disappointed to have what he perceived to be a boring gift. Then he led a mission team to South Africa. He discovered that he was the only member of the team who could keep all the details together, make all the connections, and be sure that the pieces fit together. He realized that without his gift, the rest of the team members would have been lost and confused. Without his gift, their gifts would not have been able to function. His discovery also demonstrated the truth of Paul's assertion that every gift—even the ones we don't think we want—are absolutely essential for the church to be effective in its ministry to the world.

Example #3: The Right Reason for Saying No

When I asked a business woman to lead one of our administrative committees, she said, "No." It wasn't because she didn't have the ability to do it or because she wasn't interested; it was because she had been given a vision for a new caregivers' sanctuary ministry that would meet the needs of persons who were providing support for relatives with Alzheimer's disease. She said, "When I'm doing this ministry, it makes my heart sing." Her story demonstrates the joy that a disciple experiences when God connects our gifts and passion with some specific part of the world's need. If she had been the kind of person who can't say no to the preacher, she would have ended up in a place of service that neither accomplished the mission God had prepared for her nor filled her life with joy.

"I don't know what your destiny will be, but one thing I know: the only ones among you who will be really happy are those who have sought and found how to serve."
—Albert Schweitzer[9]

In their own ways, each of these disciples had discovered their gifts and released them for ministry, and they were finding joy in being a part of God's work through them. When that happens, it's enough to make any tone-deaf person sing!

Gifts of the Kingdom

But someone will ask, "What if it doesn't work? What if my serving doesn't seem to make a difference? What then?"

Both the Gospels and the *Discipline* set our service in the context of our prayer for God's kingdom to come and God's will to be done on earth as it is in heaven. That kingdom is both here and coming. It is here in the lives and service of the followers of Jesus, and it is coming in its fullness at the final coming of Jesus Christ. The *Discipline* says that we live our lives of discipleship "in active expectancy . . . waiting for the fulfillment of God's universal love, justice, and peace on earth as in heaven."[10]

Through the power of the Holy Spirit, our servant-shaped lives become tangible expressions of God's reign and rule in the present, bearing witness to the way the world will be when God's kingdom purpose is fully accomplished in the future. We do what we do as disciples of Jesus Christ, not because we think our efforts will result in success, but because it is who we are. What we do is the direct expression of who we are.

Do you ever wonder whether the little acts of service that you offer make any difference at all? Some of us grew up hearing that it is better to light just one little candle than to stumble in the dark, but do you ever feel that "this little light of mine" just isn't much light at all?

That's how Bonaro Overstreet felt. Her poem "Stubborn Ounces" is addressed "To One Who Doubts the Worth of Doing Anything If You Can't Do Everything." She knows that the little efforts she makes don't appear to be large enough to tip the scale when justice hangs in the balance. She admits she never thought they would. But she responds by saying that she is "prejudiced beyond debate" with regard to her right to choose "which side shall feel the stubborn ounces of my weight."[11]

Sometimes the problems seem so big and the solutions seem so small. Sometimes the little bit of good that good people do seems insignificant compared to the challenges of megaproblems such as poverty, the effects of racism, and the pandemic of HIV-AIDS.

But just about the time we are ready to throw in the towel, we meet a faithful follower of Christ who finds great joy in knowing that his or her efforts, talents, resources, and gifts were being used by God to make a difference in the lives of the people whom he or she serves. People who are willing to do what they can do also choose to give what they can give, trusting that by the spirit of God it will become a part of God's transformation of this world into the kingdom of God.

Esther of the Old Testament was like that. Her story is filled with political corruption, male sexism, anti-Semitism, violence, dishonesty, and death. In other words, it was a lot like our world today. The Jews were facing the threat of extermination. Their only hope was in the hands of a young woman named Esther who, by a strange turn of events, had become the queen of Persia.

Esther's uncle, Mordecai, urged her to plead with the king for the lives of her people. The only problem was that anyone who went into the king's presence without being invited faced the possibility of death. That's when Mordecai asked a question that echoes down through time: "Who knows? Perhaps you have come to royal dignity for just such a time as this" (Esther 4:14).

She knew that her time had come. It was her time to do what she could do. With no way of knowing whether her little efforts would make any difference at all, she went to the king. Because of her efforts, the people were saved, and the Jews have been celebrating the Feast of Purim ever since.

The truth about your life and mine is that we never really know how God might use the gifts of service we offer. But we dare to believe that the spirit of God can take our lives, talents, gifts, and service and use them as a part of God's transformation of some small part of this world into something like the kingdom of God.

Evidently, God's idea of a good time is to accomplish God's saving purpose in this world through ordinary people like Esther who discover their gifts and release them for God's work in the world. The challenge for every follower of Christ is to use the gift that God has given, trusting that God will use it in ways beyond our imagination.

Some gifts are obvious while other gifts easily could go unnoticed, but they are just as important for the body of Christ to function.

I remember a woman who sat in the back row in the sanctuary every Sunday morning in the little church I served in a rural community in north central Florida. She was a tough, outspoken, independent woman who had had multiple divorces and lived in a big old house on the lake. The truth is that she didn't much like most of the people in the church, and most of the people in the church didn't much like her. But she was there in worship every Sunday.

As I got to know her, I discovered that she had what the New Testament calls the "gift of administration." She could really get things in order, as long as it didn't involve working with other people.

I mentioned one day that my sermon files were a mess. That was all she needed to hear. She went to work and created a filing system that cross-checked the sermons by scripture text, subject, and where it had been preached. She cleaned up my existing files and created new ones.

Every couple of weeks I took her a pile of file folders with my ragged manuscripts. She typed up the manuscripts, made the files, and brought them back to the office, which resulted in some pretty interesting discussions. She never hesitated to let me know when her interpretation of Scripture differed from mine.

When I left that church to start a new one, she offered to keep doing it because she knew a church-owned typewriter was not available there, and because she was afraid that somebody else would mess it up. For thirteen years I sent those boxes of sermon files to her, and she sent them back to me. She was still doing it when I came to the church I serve now, and she kept doing it until her health made it impossible for her to continue. She's in heaven now, but my guess is that if anybody messes up those sermon files, her ghost will come back to haunt me!

The point is that she discovered her gift. She released that gift in ministry, and God has been using it ever since. It was as if she had been called for just such a time as this.

In the story of Esther, there was a powerful sense of urgency. It was a life-or-death deal. The survival of the Jewish people hung in the balance, depending on her decision. Likewise, there is urgency about the decisions we make about the use of our gifts.

There are children who may never hear the stories of Jesus if people with the gift of teaching do not teach them.

There are lost, confused, spiritually searching people who may never experience God's love unless people with the gift of evangelism share the good news with them.

There are adults who may never grow in their understanding of Scripture until someone with the gift of discernment guides them.

There are people who may never find their way into the church until people with the gift of hospitality welcome them.

There are people with broken hearts and broken lives who may never find healing until people with the gift of intercession pray for them.

There are new opportunities for new ministries that may never be accomplished unless people with the gift of leadership show others the way.

There are lonely, isolated people who may never find their way into Christian community until people with the gift of mercy extend care to them.

There are important issues of justice and peace that never will be confronted until people with the gift of prophecy confront them.

In short, God has work to be done in this world that will not get done until we offer the stubborn ounces of our weight to make it happen. Who knows if we have not been created, called, and gifted for just such a time as this?

Chapter 6

The Way of Witness
Invitational Evangelism

I knew it was time to upgrade to a smartphone when the younger, more technologically savvy members of our church staff began laughing every time I pulled out my flip-top phone. I soon discovered that there were lots of options from which to choose. I learned about Android, iPhones, and Blackberries. I talked with salespersons at AT&T, T-Mobile, Verizon, and Sprint. It was more than a little baffling to me.

When I mentioned my confusion around the lunch table in the office workroom, I was suddenly besieged by staff members who passionately shared their love for their iPhone or iPad. That's when it struck me: What if people were as comfortable or as energetic sharing their relationship with Christ as they are about telling others about their iPhones?

That's a good example of what it means to be a witness. You might call it "smartphone evangelism."

Evangelism is a good word with a bad reputation. The term has been so abused by slick preachers and manipulative politicians that people inside the church are afraid to speak it and people outside the church run for cover the moment they hear it. The feeling was captured by the bumper sticker that says, "Jesus save me . . . from some of your followers!"

Evangelism comes from the root word meaning "good news." An evangelist is simply a person who shares good news.

- When was the last time you had some good news to share?
- When did you see a movie or read a book you enjoyed so much that you couldn't wait to tell someone about it?
- When did you have a great meal at a new restaurant, and you couldn't wait to take a friend there to experience it?
- When did you experience love so deep or joy so great that your first response was to invite someone else to experience it?

When we have good news, we want to share it; we want to invite someone else to experience

> "Good evangelists . . . are people who engage others in good conversation about important and profound topics. . . . They live with a sense of mission that their God-given calling in life is not just to live selfishly, or even just to live well, but to live unselfishly and well *and* to help others live unselfishly and well too. . . . They want to change the world."
>
> —Brian McLaren[1]

what we have experienced. That's evangelism, whether we use that label or not. By far the most effective form of evangelism is always personal, similar to the way one friend tells another friend about the iPhone.

Person-to-Person Witness

The diary of Benjamin Ingham demonstrates the way Oxford Methodism spread through personal witness as students shared with one another their discovery of the practices that would lead toward a holy life. Ingham records his conversations with fellow students he invited into the Wesleyan way of discipleship.

In the same way, Methodism swept across the American frontier by person-to-person witness and through the passionate preaching by the circuit riders. The early Methodists in both England and America were driven by a nearly insatiable desire to share the love of God they had experienced in Christ with anyone and everyone they could find. Although they seldom used the word *evangelism* to describe it, inviting others to experience God's love through their personal witness was the typical pattern for Wesley's followers.

In "The Character of a Methodist," John Wesley declared that Methodists "do good to all people" in every way they can. He was emphatic in saying that this went beyond meeting their physical needs for food and clothing. It meant that Methodists "do good to their souls" by inviting them to experience the love of God in Christ and by encouraging those who have experienced that love to continue to grow in their discipleship.[2]

An objective observer describing the character of a United Methodist today would probably say that we continue to "do good" in meeting many of the very real needs of people around us. When hurricanes, tornadoes, or other disasters occur, we respond. Many United Methodist congregations provide food for the hungry or shelter for the homeless. Wesley would be pleased about that. What's often missing is a Wesleyan passion for introducing spiritually searching people to new life in Jesus Christ and inviting them to join us on the pathway of discipleship. What's often missing is the kind of evangelistic desire to "do good to their souls" that reverberates through Charles Wesley's hymn when he wrote:

> *O that the world might taste and see*
> *the riches of his grace!*
> *The arms of love that compass me*
> *would all the world embrace.*[3]

Peter Storey, former Methodist bishop in South Africa, wrote that it was said of the early Methodists that anyone who worked beside them in a factory or in the coal mines was "always at risk of 'getting converted,' because [the Methodists] were so clear about this need in every life." He went on to ask, "Would that be true of us today?"[4]

Another way of asking the question might be: If Christianity were as infectious as the flu, would anyone catch it from you?

In 2008 the General Conference of The United Methodist Church added the word witness to our membership vows to underscore the importance of each individual disciple sharing the love of God with others. The need for adding that term also reflected the general loss of that kind of Wesleyan passion across much of our denomination, particularly in the United States. It prompts several challenging questions.

- What do words such as *evangelism* and *witness* mean for United Methodists today?
- What would it take for us to recover a Wesleyan passion for sharing the love of God in Christ with people outside the walls of the church?
- What part does the spiritual discipline of witness play in helping each disciple grow into a life that is centered in loving God and loving others?

The way to begin answering those questions is by seeing what evangelism looked like in the New Testament.

Evangelism in the New Testament

We could call the entire New Testament an "evangelistic" document. The word *gospel* means "good news." John says that his Gospel was written so that people would believe that Jesus is the Son of God and find life in him (John 20:30-31). The book of Acts is the energetic account of the way the good news spread through the witness of the early church. Most of the epistles are the explanation of the gospel or the application of the good news to daily life. The New Testament reaches its climax in the Revelation, which declares the good news that in spite of all evidence to the contrary, Jesus Christ is "the ruler of the kings of the earth" (Revelation 1:5). The book concludes with the invitation for everyone who is thirsty to come and receive the "water of life as a gift" (Revelation 22:17). "Witness" to Jesus Christ and "evangelism" in the sense of inviting others to experience new life in him are woven into the fabric of the New Testament.

We'll look at two examples of New Testament evangelism. First, we'll see the way that Jesus practiced evangelism. Then we'll see what it meant for Paul to be a witness for Christ.

In the opening scenes of the Gospel according to John, we meet two disciples of John the Baptist. The fact that they had been following this rugged prophet in the wilderness is a clear sign of a divine discontent in their lives—a spiritual hunger for a deeper relationship with God. Jesus offered them a simple invitation, "Come and see" (John 1:39). After spending the day with Jesus, Andrew sought out his brother, Simon, and shared the good news: "We have found the Messiah" (John 1:41). The same pattern was repeated the next day when Philip offered the same invitation to Nathanael: "Come and see" (John 1:46).

In both cases, there was no pressure or manipulation—just the simple invitation to "come and see" the one who became the answer to the searching that was already going on in their lives.

John records a similar story when Jesus meets a Samaritan woman beside Jacob's well (John 4:1-30). The story begins with an ordinary conversation about Jesus' need for a drink of water to quench his thirst. By the time the story ends, the woman has discovered "living water" and runs off to share her witness with everyone she can find.

Watch the way Jesus engaged in conversation with people in the Gospels and you will discover that Jesus-style evangelism looks like

- conversation rather than confrontation
- invitation rather than invasion
- an adventure rather than an argument
- a meeting of the hearts rather than the making of a point
- personal discovery rather than vigorous debate

Practicing Jesus-style evangelism is a people-loving, life-giving contrast to negative images of evangelism that saturate our culture today. It begins with the need in the lives of others and invites them to find the thing for which they have been searching. The Apostle Paul's example challenges us with the model of a person who was willing to do whatever it takes to share that gift.

In his letter to the Ephesians, Paul called himself "an ambassador in chains" (Ephesians 6:20), "a prisoner for Christ Jesus" (Ephesians 3:1), and a "prisoner in the Lord" (Ephesians 4:1). At the time he wrote this letter, it was literally true—and it is literally true for many Christians in the world today. Throughout Christian history, being faithful to the gospel often has meant being on a collision course with what Paul called "the principalities and powers" of the world.

What's amazing is Paul's response to his imprisonment. He didn't moan or complain. He didn't plead or protest the injustice of it. Instead, he gave thanks for the calling that got him into trouble:

> "You have nothing to do but to save souls. Therefore spend and be spent in this work. And go always, not only to those who want [i.e., need] you, but to those who want you most."
>
> —John Wesley[5]

Of this gospel I have become a servant according to the gift of God's grace that was given me by the working of his power. Although I am the very least of all the saints, this grace was given to me to bring to the Gentiles the news of the boundless riches of Christ. (Ephesians 3:7-8)

In his letter to the Philippians, Paul wrote that his imprisonment had "actually helped to spread the gospel" (1:12). He surprises us by asking, "What does it matter? Just this, that Christ is proclaimed in every way . . . and in that I rejoice" (1:18).

Now, that's amazing! Paul's passion for sharing the love of God in Christ was so strong, and his joy in seeing the difference Christ makes in the lives of those who find him was so deep, that it outweighed any suffering, any injustice, any embarrassment, or any pain that he experienced. Nothing mattered as much to Paul as sharing the good news of God's love in Christ with anyone and everyone he could find.

When you think about the great good news that Paul had to share—the good news of God's love in Christ—what's really amazing is that we are often so hesitant to share it.

Becoming a Witness for Jesus Christ

After forty years of pastoral ministry, one of the deepest convictions of my life is that there is a significant number of unchurched, uncommitted people in our world who long to experience the love of God through a grace-centered faith tradition. For many of these individuals, the most appropriate way to experience God's love and grace and become a disciple of Jesus Christ is through the center flow of the Wesleyan spiritual tradition. When they finally do experience the gospel in the context of our tradition, their first response often is something similar to "Where have you been all my life?" It's as if they have been waiting for a faithful Methodist disciple to say, "Come and see."

With Paul, I rejoice wherever Christ is made known. I know that some folks are wired to experience the gospel the way Baptist or Catholic or Presbyterian or Pentecostal churches share it. But I also know that a huge slice of the population around us, whether realizing it or not, is just waiting for the invitation to experience the love of God in the center flow of our spiritual and theological tradition.

I was leading our Pastor's Coffee a few weeks after we completed a worship series that focused on the Wesleyan understanding of grace. Each person in the circle was sharing how he or she had ended up at Hyde Park. One young woman, with tears in her eyes, said that the Sunday I preached on prevenient grace was her first day here. She said that although she had never heard that term before, it was the message she had been waiting to hear all of her life. I had the joy of baptizing her into the faith as the expression of her new commitment to Jesus Christ, and like Andrew, she immediately started inviting people around her to experience what she found.

Most of us desire to be like this enthusiastic woman, but sometimes we struggle with knowing *how* to share our faith with others. How can we practice Jesus-style evangelism? What practical steps along the discipleship pathway will enable us to become a witness for Jesus Christ? Here are a few suggestions.

> "We cannot expect the wanderers from God to seek us. It is our part to go and seek them."
> —Charles Wesley[6]

Begin with friendship. No one wants to be manipulated. Evangelism that is centered in Christlike love for others begins in honest, nonmanipulative, life-giving human friendships. The challenge for many church folks is that all of our friends are already followers of Christ. How many friendships do you have with people who do not yet know Christ?

Listen. Listen. Listen. It's easy to begin with the assumption that witnessing is all about telling someone about Christ. But Jesus' relationship with Andrew began with a question: "What are you looking for?" (John 1:38). In his conversation with the Samaritan woman at the well, Jesus listened deeply to the thirst in her soul (John 4:1-30). Are you more interested in listening to another's person's story than in sharing your own?

Know your story. The attorneys in my congregation have taught me that in the courtroom, the role of witnesses is not to argue the case or to judge the outcome but simply to tell what they heard, saw, and experienced. Whenever the opportunity came, the apostles were ready to tell the story of the way they met Christ and the difference he had made in their lives. Can you tell the story of your relationship with Christ in a simple, clear, and concise way?

Offer the invitation. The invitation to "come and see" can take whatever form is appropriate to the situation. It may be a direct invitation to make a commitment to Christ. It may be an invitation to visit your church, to join a small group, or to participate in some form of mission or ministry. It is always an open-ended invitation that begins a journey toward a Christ-centered life.

Trust the Spirit. Because we believe in prevenient grace, we believe that the love of God is already at work in people's lives before they are even aware of it. They may be more ready than you realize. We can trust the Spirit to prepare the way, to be at work in the relationship, to open the right conversation at the right time, and to give us the right way to respond.

The bottom line is that being a witness isn't nearly as difficult or intimidating as it often seems. It simply means being who we are as followers of Jesus Christ and allowing the spirit of God to use our lives to touch the lives of others.

When I think about what it means to be a witness for Jesus Christ, I recall a beautiful e-mail message in which a new disciple recounted the steps that led her along the way.

The journey began when a friend told her about the difference that Christ was making in her life and invited her to our church. The writer of the e-mail responded to the invitation and reported that she experienced love and understanding—not guilt and shame—in our worship. She reminded me of the Samaritan woman when she said that she left each Sunday feeling refreshed and thirsty for more.

The next step was when she responded to an invitation to try one of our small groups. In that group she not only learned to study the Bible and pray; she said that she also found "good friends and a few great friends—all friends in Christ."

Along the way she was encouraged to discover her gifts and find ways to use those gifts in ministry to others. She described the joy she experienced in giving herself to others and thanked me for the opportunity of serving through the church.

All of this was happening in her life before she came to the Pastor's Coffee and entered into the new member process that led toward taking the vows of membership. By then she, like the Samaritan woman, had already become a witness to others. After she became a member of the church, she sent me an e-mail in which she reflected on the ways her life had changed. She said it was "just plain fun" to tell her friends about the ways she was involved in the mission

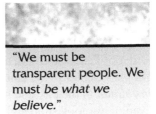

"We must be transparent people. We must *be what we believe.*"
—Peter Storey[7]

of the church. She particularly enjoyed seeing the look of surprise on the faces of business acquaintances when she answered the question "What are you up to these days?" She celebrated the way she was able to persevere when things got rough because of her new-found life in Christ.

Now, that's what I call Jesus-style evangelism!

Practicing Whole-life Witness

Here's the challenge. Our witness for Christ is never complete if it touches only individual lives. As Methodists, we believe that we are called to go into the world with a whole-life witness. In other words, our witness should transform not only the lives of individuals but also the world in which we live. In this way our witness becomes an expression of the kingdom of God, coming on earth as it is already fulfilled in heaven.

Sometimes individual Christians and churches tend to emphasize either personal witness on the one hand or social witness on the other, but whole-life evangelism binds both together in a life-transforming whole. Speaking out of his experience as a pastor and a leader in the struggle against apartheid, Peter Storey calls for an end to "the sterile debate" between personal and social witness in his book *With God in the Crucible.* Describing Christians who focus only on a personal gospel, he writes, "For such people the Kingdom reaches no further than the conversion of the individual soul. Their God is too small to transform the world." Then he points to Christians whose witness is focused solely on social, political, and economic systems, saying, "Their God is too busy to heal a wounded soul."[8] Storey describes the two sides as castaways on a deserted island. One holds a can of food and one holds a can opener, but both go hungry because they think they do not need the other.

Storey's solution is a relentless call for "prophetic evangelism." His words and his life demonstrate a way of witness that is evangelical enough to call for personal conversion to transform the evil in the unredeemed soul while at the same time being bold enough to confront the evil that penetrates the economic systems and political structures of our world as we participate with God in the work of social justice and transformation.[9]

The combination of personal and social witness was marked indelibly on my soul a number of years ago when I was guest preacher at Central Methodist Mission in downtown Johannesburg, South Africa. In the evening we went out knocking on apartment doors in the overcrowded flats that filled the inner city, praying with people and inviting them to the church. In the morning we stood with the Methodist Order of Peacemakers in a protest against military conscription. We ate lunch in the People's Center in the church basement, which at that time was the only nonracial restaurant in the city and served as a persistent witness against apartheid. In the evening we took soup and bread to homeless people who were spending the night on the streets.

That kind of whole-life witness is in the center flow of the Methodist tradition. Along with his call to a transformed life, John Wesley called for the transformation of the social structures of his time by confronting issues of poverty, economic injustice, imprisonment, and war.

Wesley continued the call for social reform until the end of his life. In fact, the last letter he wrote was to William Wilberforce, who had been converted through the Wesleyan Revival. In the letter Wesley encouraged Wilberforce to continue his struggle for the abolition of slavery, writing with the same passion he expressed when sharing his personal faith in Christ. Wesley died just six days later on March 2, 1791. The struggle went on for sixteen years until Parliament abolished the slave trade in 1807.

United Methodist congregations today that are fulfilling the mission of making disciples for the transformation of the world practice a Wesleyan expression of whole-life witness. In ways that are uniquely matched to the communities they serve, they are inviting people to active discipleship in a transforming relationship with Jesus Christ while also reaching out to the needs of the community around them. Here are a few examples:

- A retirement community congregation is vigorously evangelistic in calling people to new life in Christ while providing recovery ministries that touch hundreds of lives every week.
- An aging, urban center congregation is making radical changes in its style of ministry to reach the diverse population around it while providing showers for homeless people and aggressively bearing witness to the need for social justice in the church, city, and nation.
- A congregation in a middle- to upper-class neighborhood has seen major growth in its membership while becoming a model for ministry with homeless people and a witness for Christian nonviolence and peace.
- A megachurch reaches out to a major city through a wide array of practical services to demonstrate that "salvation isn't just about the hereafter. God wants us to prosper holistically today and to help others go and do likewise."[10]

Both as individuals and as congregations, the people called Methodists are called to whole-life witness by which growing disciples of Jesus Christ become a part of God's transformation of the world. When Jesus said, "You shall be my witnesses" (Acts 1:8), he wasn't speaking only to the first apostles. He was speaking to us!

POSTSCRIPT

On the Journey

I wonder whether Benjamin Ingham had any idea what he was getting into when he made his way through Oxford to meet with John Wesley on that brisk spring morning in 1734?

We know he was experiencing a "divine discontent"—a nagging hunger for a life that was more fully aligned with the way of life revealed in Jesus Christ. My guess is that, steeped in the Anglican tradition, Ingham would have been familiar with the prayer of Saint Richard of Chichester (1197–1253):

> O most merciful Redeemer, friend and brother,
> May I know Thee more clearly,
> Love Thee more dearly,
> Follow Thee more nearly.[1]

Ingham came to Wesley for practical guidance on how to practice the time-tested disciplines that would lead him to a "holy life." By coming to Wesley, he had come to the right place.

John and Charles Wesley guided Ingham and his friends along a path of methodical discipleship that resulted in more:

- disciplined life of *prayer* and Scripture
- faithful *presence* in worship and in community with other disciples
- radical generosity in the stewardship of their financial *gifts*
- energetic giving of their lives in *service* to others, and
- courageous *witness* that would invite others to experience the love of God in Christ

Through the consistent practice of these spiritual disciplines, the lives of the early Methodists were transformed, and they became a part of God's transformation of the world.

Now the invitation comes to us from the risen Christ, "Follow me!" As disciples of Jesus Christ in The United Methodist Church, we have the challenge to take our next appropriate step along the path that will lead in the direction of a life that is centering in loving God and loving others. How will we respond?

In his book *The Life You've Always Wanted*, John Ortberg makes a helpful distinction between trying and training. He says that anyone can try to run a marathon, but only those who train for it will actually accomplish it.[2]

In the same way, anyone can *try* to be a follower of Christ, but the only people who actually discover the life to which God has called us are those who *train* for it. Ortberg concludes, "Spiritual transformation is not a matter of trying harder, but of training wisely"[3] Disciples are people who choose to enter into the spiritual disciplines that, if practiced over time, will enable them to become

Spirit-energized, grace-filled, joy-soaked disciples who are learning to love God with their whole hearts, souls, minds, and strength while learning to love others the way they have been loved by God.

We know what the practices are; we affirm them when members are received into The United Methodist Church. We are called to the constant recommitment of our prayers, presence, gifts, service, and witness. They are the *methods* by which Methodist people are formed into the likeness of Christ and become the agents of his kingdom in this world.

The persistent question is the degree to which we are willing to commit and recommit ourselves to the practice of the disciplines.

In his *Journal* and again in his *Short History of the People Called Methodists*, John Wesley (1781) described the first "covenant service." It was designed as a time for Methodist people to renew the commitments that bind them in covenant with God. The first covenant service was held on August 11, 1755, with eighteen hundred people present. It soon became the custom of British Methodists to use the Covenant Service in "Watchnight" services on New Year's Eve as a way of renewing their commitment to Christ at the beginning of the new year. In 1780, Wesley published the basic order for the service that continues to be used by Methodist people around the world today.

The climax of the Covenant Service is a prayer that captures the radical commitment of the early Methodists and continues to challenge us in our commitments today. I can think of no better way to commit ourselves to our next step along the path of discipleship than to offer this prayer:

> I am no longer my own but yours. Put me to what you will, rank me with whom you will. Put me to doing, put me to suffering. Let me be employed for you or laid aside for you, exalted for you or brought low for you. Let me be full, let me be empty. Let me have all things, let me have nothing. I freely and wholeheartedly yield all things to your pleasure and disposal.
>
> And now, glorious and blessed God, Father, Son, and Holy Spirit, you are mine and I am yours. So be it. And the covenant now made on earth, let it be ratified in heaven. Amen.[4]

Continuing the Journey

Recommended Resources

Discipleship in the Wesleyan tradition never ends. It is a continuing journey of faith in which we are "changed from glory into glory, 'till in heaven we take our place" ("Love Divine, All Loves Excelling," *The United Methodist Hymnal,* 384). The good news is that the resources for continued growth in grace are inexhaustible. The following are a few recommended works for continued discovery along the discipleship pathway in our rich Wesleyan tradition.

Paul Wesley Chilcote, *John & Charles Wesley: Selections from their Writings and Hymns—Annotated & Explained* (Skylight Paths Publishing, 2011). Paul Chilcote provides a very accessible introduction to the Wesleys through an excellent summary of their lives and helpful insights into their words and hymns.

James A. Harnish, *Simple Rules for Money: John Wesley on Earning, Saving, and Giving* (Abingdon Press, 2010). Guided by the Bible and the timeless wisdom of John Wesley, James A. Harnish challenges Christians to face the issue of money head-on, with God's help.

Steve Harper, *The Way to Heaven: The Gospel According to John Wesley* (Zondervan, 2003). Steve Harper makes the core affirmations of Wesley's theology easily understood by laypersons in a non-academic setting.

Richard P. Heitzenrater, *Wesley and the People Called Methodist* (Abingdon Press, 1995). Richard Heitzenrater is one of the most highly respected Wesley scholars in the world today. Out of a lifetime of saturation in the Wesleyan tradition, his account of the birth of the Wesleyan movement invites the reader to claim that tradition as his or her own.

Reuben P. Job, *A Wesleyan Spiritual Reader* (Abingdon, 1997). Bishop Job designs a pattern for personal devotion and prayer based on the words of Wesley and other writers in the Wesleyan tradition.

J. Ellsworth Kalas, *Our First Song: Evangelism in the Hymns of Charles Wesley* (Discipleship Resources, 1984, reprinted by Asbury Theological Seminary, 2007). Ellsworth Kalas captures both the themes and feelings of the hymns by which Wesleyan theology sang its way into the hearts of the Methodist people.

Andy and Sally Langford, *Living as United Methodist Christians* (Abingdon, 2011). Out of their pastoral experience, the Langfords help contemporary United Methodists claim the beliefs and unique emphases of discipleship in the Wesleyan tradition.

NOTES

Introduction: A Divine Discontent

1. Richard Heitzenrater, *Diary of an Oxford Methodist* (Durham, N.C.: Duke University Press, 1985), 2.
2. See Richard Heitzenrater, *John Wesley and the People Called Methodists* (Nashville: Abingdon, 1995), ix.
3. See "The Baptismal Covenant" (I–IV), in *The United Methodist Hymnal* (Nashville: The United Methodist Publishing House, 1989), 38. Also see http/content3://www.gbod.org/site/apps/nlnet.aspx?c=nhLRJ2PMKsG&b=5657895&ct=7778669.
4. Frank Whaling, ed., *John and Charles Wesley: Selected Prayers, Hymns, Journal Notes, Sermons, Letters, and Treatises* (Mahwah, N.J.: Paulist Press, 1981), 205.

Why Are You a United Methodist?

1. *Time*, March 12, 2009, http://www.time.com/time/specials/packages/article/0,28804, 1884779_1884782_1884760,00.html (accessed October 10, 2011).
2. Ibid.
3. William Paul Young, *The Shack* (Newbury Park, Calif.: Windblown Media, 2007), 185.
4. Charles Wesley, "Come, Sinners, to the Gospel Feast," in *The United Methodist Hymnal* (Nashville: The United Methodist Publishing House, 1989), 339.
5. Charles Wesley, "O for a Heart to Praise My God," in *The United Methodist Hymnal* (Nashville: The United Methodist Publishing House, 1989), 417.
6. http://en.wikiquote.org/wiki/John_Wesley (accessed September 6, 2011).
7. Peter Storey, *And Are We Yet Alive? Revisioning Our Wesleyan Heritage in a New Southern Africa* (Cape Town: Methodist Publishing House, 2004), 37.
8. John Wesley, "Christian Perfection," http://new.gbgm-umc.org/umhistory/wesley/sermons/40/ (accessed August 29, 2011).
9. John Wesley, "The Character of a Methodist," http://new.gbgm-umc.org/umhistory/wesley/character/ (accessed August 29, 2011).
10. Ibid.
11. *The Book of Discipline of The United Methodist Church, 2008* (Nashville: The United Methodist Publishing House, 2008), 41.
12. "The Apostles' Creed, Traditional Version," in *The United Methodist Hymnal* (Nashville: The United Methodist Publishing House, 1989), 881.
13. The *Discipline*, 43.
14. Ibid.
15. Ibid.
16. Ibid., 45–46.
17. http://en.wikipedia.org/wiki/Anglican_sacraments (accessed August 25, 2011).
18. John Wesley, "The Duty of Constant Communion," http://new.gbgm-umc.org/umhistory/wesley/sermons/101/ (accessed October 10, 2011).
19. Charles Wesley, "Come, Sinners, to the Gospel Feast," in *The United Methodist Hymnal* (Nashville: The United Methodist Publishing House, 1989), 616.

20. The *Discipline*, 90.

21. Ibid., 87.

22. Ibid.

Chapter 1: Discipleship in the Way of Grace: A Disciple's Path Defined

1. Lewis Carroll, *The Annotated Alice*, introduction by Martin Gardner (New York: W. W. Norton, 2000), 65.

2. Heitzenrater, *Diary of an Oxford Methodist*, 36.

3. John Wesley, "On Zeal," http://new.gbgm-umc.org/umhistory/wesley/sermons/92/ (accessed August 29, 2011).

4. Friedrich Nietzsche, *Beyond Good and Evil*, quoted in Eugene Peterson, *A Long Obedience in the Same Direction* (Downers Grove, Ill.: InterVarsity Press, 1980), 13.

5. John Newton, "Amazing Grace," in *The United Methodist Hymnal* (Nashville: Abingdon Press, 1989), 378.

6. Kenneth J. Collins, *The Scripture Way of Salvation* (Nashville: Abingdon Press, 1997), 19.

7. Francis Thompson, "The Hound of Heaven," http://www.bartleby.com/236/239.html (accessed August 29, 2011).

8. Rueben Job, *A Wesleyan Reader* (Nashville: Abingdon Press, 1998), 159.

9. Charles Wesley, "Stupendous Love of God Most High," http://www.poemhunter.com /poem/hymn-xxv-stupendous-love-of-god-most-high/ (accessed August 29, 2011).

10. Arthur Miller, *Death of a Salesman*, in *The Portable Arthur Miller* (New York: Penguin, 1995), 125–26.

11. "I Sought the Lord," in *The Book of Hymns* (Nashville: Board of Publication of The Methodist Church, 1966), 96.

12. John E. Booty, ed., *John Donne: Selections from Divine Poems, Sermons, Devotions, and Prayers* (New York: Paulist Press, 1990), p. 58.

13. John Wesley, "On Sin in Believers," http://new.gbgm-umc.org/umhistory/wesley/sermons/13/ (accessed August 29, 2011).

14. The *Discipline*, 46.

15. *Selections from E. Stanley Jones* (Nashville: Abingdon Press, 1972), 251.

16. Charles Wesley, "And Can It Be that I Should Gain," in *The United Methodist Hymnal* (Nashville: Abingdon Press, 1989), 363.

17. Job, *A Wesleyan Reader,* 187.

18. Charles Wesley, "Love Divine, All Loves Excelling," in *The United Methodist Hymnal* (Nashville: Abingdon Press, 1989), 384.

19. Collins, *The Scripture Way of Salvation,* 45.

Chapter 2: The Path of Biblical Prayer: Prayer and Scripture Meditation

1. Robert Kegan and Lisa Laskow Lahey, *Immunity to Change* (Boston: Harvard Business School Publishing, 2009), 1.

2. John Wesley, "The Way to the Kingdom," http://new.gbgm-umc.org/umhistory/wesley/sermons/7/ (accessed August 29, 2011).

3. Ibid.

4. Heitzenrater, *Diary of an Oxford Methodist*, 13.

5. Ibid., 105.

6. Ibid., 56.

7. Job, *A Wesleyan Spiritual Reader*, 15.

8. http://en.wikipedia.org/wiki/Wesley_Covenant_Prayer (accessed October 10, 2011).

9. http://www.step12.com/step-4.html (accessed September 14, 2011).

10. Heitzenrater, *Diary of an Oxford Methodist*, 119–20.

11. Ibid., 168–69.

12. "Devotional Life in the Wesleyan Tradition," in Job, *A Wesleyan Spiritual Reader*, 20.

13. Charles Wesley, "Soldiers of Christ, Arise," in *The United Methodist Hymnal* (Nashville: The United Methodist Publishing House, 1989), 513.

14. The *Discipline*, 44.

15. Ibid, 60.

16. Heitzenrater, *Diary of an Oxford Methodist,* 21.

17. Ibid.

18. John Wesley, "An Appeal to Men of Reason and Religion," http://www.imarc.cc/br/breckbill.html (accessed August 29, 2011).

19. The *Discipline,* 78.

20. Lewis Carroll, *The Annotated Alice*, introduction by Martin Gardner (New York: W. W. Norton, 2000), 199.

21. The *Discipline*, 81.

22. John Wesley, *Explanatory Notes Upon the Old Testament*, http://gbgm-umc.org/umw/wesley/bible.stm (accessed August 29, 2011).

23. Henri Nouwen, "A Self-Emptied Heart: The Disciplines of Spiritual Formation," *Sojourners,* August 20, 1981, 20.

Chapter 3: The Priority of Presence: Corporate Worship and Small-group Community

1. Eugene Nicholas Heidt quotation, http://www.angelusonline.org/index.php?section=articles&subsection=show_article&article_id=2577 (accessed on August 25, 2011).

2. E. Stanley Jones, speech delivered at Asbury College, Fall 1966.

3. Desmond Tutu, *No Future Without Forgiveness* (New York: Doubleday, 1999), 31.

4. *John and Charles Wesley: Selected Writings and Hymns* (Mahwah, NJ: Paulist Press, 1981),107.

5. *The Works of John Wesley,* Jackson Edition, "Preface to 1739 Hymns and Sacred Poems," 14:32, http://deeplycommitted.com/2009/02/03/wesley-said-it-the-necessity-of-social-holiness/ (accessed August 29, 2011).

6. Richard Heitzenrater, *Wesley and the People Called Methodists*, 21ff.

7. Charles Wesley, "All Praise to Our Redeeming Lord," in *The United Methodist Hymnal* (Nashville: The United Methodist Publishing House, 1989), 554.

8. Richard Heitzenrater, *Wesley and the People Called Methodists*, 113.

9. Ibid., 24–25.

10. The *Discipline,* 74.

11. John Ed Mathison, *Treasures of the Transformed Life* (Nashville: Abingdon Press, 2006), 111.

12. "Biography for Woody Allen," http://www.imdb.com/name/nm0000095/bio (accessed on September 19, 2011).

13. http://dictionary.reference.com/browse/liturgy (accessed September 6, 2011).

14. John Wesley's Journal, March 2, 1739, http://www.ccel.org/ccel/wesley /journal.vi.iii.i.html (accessed September 19, 2011).

15. Eugene Peterson, *Christ Plays in Ten Thousand Places* (Grand Rapids, Mich.: Eerdmans, 2005), 41.

16. "I Love to Tell the Story," words by A. Katherine Hankey, 1866, *The United Methodist Hymnal* (Nashville: The United Methodist Publishing House, 1989), 156.

17. See John Wesley's sermon "The Duty of Constant Communion," http://new.gbgm-umc .org/umhistory/wesley/sermons/101/ (accessed August 29, 2011).

Chapter 4: Money Matters: Financial Generosity

1. Umair Haque, "A Roadmap to Life that Matters," *Harvard Business Review*, July 13, 2011, http://blogs.hbr.org/haque/2011/07/a_roadmap_to_a_life_that.html (accessed August 26, 2011).

2. "Baptismal Covenant I," in *The United Methodist Hymnal* (Nashville: The United Methodist Publishing House, 1989), 35.

3. Haque, "A Roadmap to Life that Matters."

4. Ibid.

5. See http://new.gbgm-umc.org/umhistory/wesley/sermons/title/.

6. John Wesley, "On the Danger of Increasing Riches," http://new.gbgm-umc.org/umhistory/wesley/sermons/126/ (accessed August 26, 2011).

7. John Wesley, "The Use of Money," http://new.gbgm-umc.org/umhistory/wesley/sermons/50/ (accessed August 29, 2011).

8. Ibid.

9. Ibid.

10. Ibid.

11. Ibid.

12. Ibid.

13. http://dictionary.reference.com/browse/frugal (accessed September 12, 2011).

14. Wesley, "The Use of Money."

15. Ibid.

16. Haque, "A Roadmap to Life that Matters."

17. http://en.wikipedia.org/wiki/Collyer_brothers (accessed September 12, 2011).

18. Haque, "A Roadmap to Life that Matters."

Chapter 5: The Way of Service: Spiritual Gifts and Gifts-based Service

1. "Stradivarius Tops Auction Record," BBC News, May 17, 2006, http://news.bbc.co.uk /2/hi/entertainment/4988838.stm (accessed September 6, 2011).

2. George Eliot, "Stradivarius," in *Poems of George Eliot* (New York: Frederick Stokes, 1891), 139–43.

3. Ibid., 143.

4. Eugene Peterson, *Practice Resurrection* (Grand Rapids, Mich.: Eerdmans, 2010), 47, 49.

5. Paul Wesley Chilcote, *Recapturing the Wesleys' Vision* (Downer's Grove, Ill.: InterVarsity Press, 2004), 95.

6. The *Discipline,* 90.

7. Ibid., 89.

8. Ibid., 90.

9. http://www.goodreads.com/quotes/show/74745 (accessed October 10, 2011).

10. The *Discipline,* 91.

11. Bonaro Overstreet, "Stubborn Ounces," in *Signature* (New York: W. W. Norton, 1978), 19.

Chapter 6: The Way of Witness: Invitational Evangelism

1. Brian McLaren, *More Ready Than You Realize* (Grand Rapids: Zondervan, 2002), 14.

2. John Wesley, "The Character of a Methodist," http://new.gbgm-umc.org/umhistory/wesley/character/ (accessed September 1, 2011).

3. Charles Wesley, "Jesus! the Name High Over All," http://gbgm-umc.org/UMhistory/wesley/hymns/umh193.stm (accessed September 1, 2011).

4. Peter Storey, *And Are We Yet Alive? Revisioning Our Wesleyan Heritage in a New Southern Africa* (Cape Town: Methodist Publishing House, 2004), 50.

5. John Wesley, Minutes of the 1745 Conference, in Heitzenrater, *Wesley and the People Called Methodists,* 153.

6. Charles Wesley quoted in Heitzenrater, *Wesley and the People Called Methodists,* 162.

7. Peter Storey, *With God in the Crucible* (Nashville: Abingdon Press, 2002), 32.

8. Ibid., 153.

9. Ibid.

10. Windsor Village United Methodist Church, Houston, Texas, http://www.kingdombuilders.com/templates/cuskingdombuilders/details.asp?id=23260&PID=68419 (accessed October 10, 2011).

Postscript: On the Journey

1. http://en.wikipedia.org/wiki/Richard_of_Chichester (accessed October 10, 2011).

2. John Ortberg, *The Life You've Always Wanted* (Grand Rapids: Zondervan, 1997), 45–46.

3. Ibid., 47.

4. http://wesleyanleadership.wordpress.com/2011/01/07/the-wesley-covenant-prayer-as-a-declaration-of-missional-discipleship/ (accessed October 10. 2011).

Made in the USA
Middletown, DE
24 January 2022

59554695R00046